Passport to Tax-Free International Living

Passport to Tax-Free International Living
by Adam Starchild

Copyright © 2000 by Adam Starchild

ISBN 1-893713-11-3

Published by International Law and Taxation Publishers

London

All rights reserved, including the right to reproduce this book, or portions threof, in any form.

Contents

Introduction 1

The World as Your Home — Being a Perpetual Traveler 5
   Your Yacht — An Oceanic Home 6

The Principality of Andorra 9
   Tax Facts of Interest 10

Antigua and Barbuda 13
   History and Government 13
   The Economy of Antigua and Barbuda 14
   Tax Facts of Interest 15

Anguilla 17
   History and Government 17
   The Economy of Anguilla 18
   Tax Facts of Interest 18

Argentina 21
   History and Government 22
   The Economy of Argentina 22
   Tax Facts of Interest 23

Aruba 25
   History and Government 26
   The Economy of Aruba 27
   Tax Facts of Interest 27

The Bahamas 29
   History and Government 30
   Economy of The Bahamas 31
   Tax Facts of Interest 31

Bermuda 33
   History and Government 34
   Bermuda's Economy 35
   Tax Facts of Interest 35

Bolivia **39**
    History and Government 40
    Bolivia's Economy 41
    Tax Facts of Interest 41

Campione **43**
    History and Government 44
    The Economy of Campione 44
    Tax Facts of Interest 44

The Cayman Islands **47**
    History and Government 48
    The Economy of the Cayman Islands 48
    Tax Facts of Interest 49

Ceuta and Melilla **51**
    History and Government 52
    The Economies of Ceuta and Melilla 53
    Tax Facts of Interest 53

Costa Rica **55**
    History and Government 56
    The Economy of Costa Rica 57
    Tax Facts of Interest 58

Cyprus **59**
    History and Government 60
    The Economy of Cyprus 61
    Tax Facts of Interest 62

Dubai **65**
    History and Government 66
    The Economy of Dubai 67
    Tax Facts of Interest 67

Ecuador **71**
    History and Government 72
    The Economy of Ecuador 73
    Tax Facts of Interest 74

Greece **79**
    History and Government 80
    The Economy of Greece 81
    Tax Facts of Interest 82

Guatemala **87**
    History and Government 89
    The Economy of Guatemala 89
    Tax Facts of Interest 90

Honduras **93**
    History and Government 94
    The Economy of Honduras 95
    Tax Facts of Interest 97

Hong Kong **99**
    History and Government 100
    The Economy of Hong Kong 101
    Tax Facts of Interest 102

The Republic of Ireland **103**
    History and Government 104
    The Economy of Ireland 105
    Tax Facts of Interest 106

Israel **109**
    History and Government 110
    The Economy of Israel 111
    Tax Facts of Interest 111

Jordan **115**
    History and Government 116
    The Economy of Jordan 118
    Tax Facts of Interest 119

Malta **121**
    History and Government 122
    The Economy of Malta 123
    Tax Facts of Interest 124

Mexico **127**
    History and Government 128
    The Economy of Mexico 129
    Tax Facts of Interest 130

Monaco **133**
    History and Government 134
    The Economy of Monaco 134
    Tax Facts of Interest 135

Nicaragua **137**
    History and Government 138
    The Economy of Nicaragua 139
    Tax Facts of Interest 140

Panama **143**
    History and Government 144
    The Economy of Panama 146
    Tax Facts of Interest 146

Paraguay **149**
    History and Government 150
    The Economy of Paraguay 151
    Tax Facts of Interest 152

Philippines **153**
    History and Government 155
    The Economy of the Philippines 156
    Tax Facts of Interest 157

St. Kitts and Nevis **161**
    History and Government 162
    The Economy of St. Kitts and Nevis 163
    Tax Facts of Interest 163

St. Martin (St. Maarten) **165**
    History and Government 166
    The Economy of St. Martin 167
    Tax Facts of Interest 167

Seychelles 171
    History and Government 172
    The Economy of Seychelles 173
    Tax Facts of Interest 174

Tunisia 177
    History and Government 178
    The Economy of Tunisia 179
    Tax Facts of Interest 180

Turkey 181
    History and Government 182
    The Economy of Turkey 183
    Tax Facts of Interest 184

Turks and Caicos 187
    History and Government 188
    The Economy of the Turks and Caicos 189
    Tax Facts of Interest 189

United Kingdom 191
    History and Government 192
    The Economy of the United Kingdom 194
    Tax Facts of Interest 195

Uruguay 199
    History and Government 200
    The Economy of Uruguay 201
    Tax Facts of Interest 202

Getting A Second Citizenship 203

Some Examples of Visa-Free Travel & Residence 207

Why Your Investments Also Need To Reside In A Haven 209
    Solving The Worldwide Taxation Problem For American Citizens . 210
    Sources of Help for Offshore Investing 211

Tax-Free Investing in the United States 219
    American Options Investing 220
    Asset Allocation — The Key To Successful Investing 224

Using Canada as a Stepping Stone 233
    Canada - Number One in the World 233
    Tax Free New Canadians 235
    Becoming a Canadian 238
    Essential Preliminaries 245
    The Mechanics of Offshore Business 256
    Afterward 263
    In Conclusion 271

Go Do It! 273

About the Author 275

Introduction

If you are like most people, you undoubtedly feel that you have paid enough taxes during your career to last several lifetimes, and you certainly don't relish the idea of paying taxes once you are retired. You may not have to. There are places around the world offering outstanding lifestyles that you can enjoy during your retirement (or even semi-retirement) where you may considerably reduce the taxes you would expect to pay in your home country. In some places you may be able to eliminate income taxes entirely. The opportunities exist; they are even promoted by some jurisdictions.

These places may be thought of as *retirement havens*, which is the subject of this book. Simply put, a retirement haven is a country, jurisdiction, or city that offers special tax incentives for their residents. While such places may be attractive to various individuals, they are especially so for retirees who wish to maintain their assets in the safest and most efficient manner possible. Unquestionably, one of the most effective methods for maintaining assets during the retirement years is to reduce your tax burden.

Before you read any further in this book, be advised that the author does not endorse any retirement haven over another. Included in the pages that follow are places around the world that may prove suitable for individuals who are retired, or are about to retire, and who wish to significantly reduce their tax burden in a land that is pleasant, safe, and where they can enjoy a superior style of life. The golden years can truly be golden with proper planning and wise decision-making.

You may find that you wish not to move to another part of the world during your retirement, or that you don't wish to live in any particular place. Perhaps you wish to travel the world perpetually. There is a term for this —

Residence Havens

Perpetual Traveler. Indeed there are people who have retired and bought yachts that they use as an "ocean-going mobile home." They visit ports and magnificent cities throughout the world, remaining for the length of time the country allows (which may be several months), and then sailing to the next destination. By not being a "resident" of a country, you are not liable for taxes. The sophistication of personal computers and internet data links can keep you in touch with the world and informed about your investments.

Before you decide to relocate to any place, you should find as much information about the area and country as you can. While this book provides basic facts about potential retirement havens, it should be viewed only as a guide that points you in possible directions. Further investigation on your part, including visiting the place for an extended stay in which you have a chance to learn about the area, its people, and its opportunities, are strongly advised.

To make a sound decision on a retirement haven, you should consider many factors, including:

- **GEOGRAPHY.** Do you like the physical surroundings? Do you like this part of the world? Are you close enough to relatives and friends should you, or they, wish to visit? How accessible is this place to other cities and countries? Is there adequate air and sea transport? Does the land offer the types of activities you enjoy — fishing, swimming, hiking, skiing, etc.?

- **CLIMATE.** Is the climate agreeable to you? A person who enjoys the change of the seasons typical to a temperate climate may not like the year-round summer of a tropical island. (On the other hand, that person may desire to retire in the sun.) Be sure to take into account the amount of rainfall, humidity, and temperature variations of each locale you are considering.

- **LIFESTYLE.** What type of lifestyle can you enjoy in this retirement haven? Does it have adequate, or better yet, excellent health care? Is it safe, being relatively crime free? Does it have a modern infrastructure, meaning that you will be able to enjoy an up-to-date telecommunications

Introduction

system, utilities, and transportation system? What is the housing like? Will you be able to find comfortable, affordable housing?

- **GOVERNMENT.** What type of government does the retirement haven possess? How stable is the government? Are you comfortable with it?

- **ECONOMY.** What type of economy does the retirement haven have? Is it diversified and strong? Will you need to invest in the economy in order to enjoy special tax incentives? Will your investments be safe? What is the long-term outlook for the economy. Can you expect sustained growth?

These and similar questions must be answered if you are to enjoy your life of retirement and benefit from the advantages a retirement haven has to offer. No two retirement havens are alike. Each has unique characteristics that individuals must evaluate according to their own likes, dislikes, and expectations.

Retirement need not be a mundane affair in which you watch your hard-earned savings and investments dwindle away due to a high cost of living and burdensome taxes. With the proper planning it can be a time of new opportunities and enjoyment, as well as a time in which you keep more of your assets by reducing your cost of living and taxes.

The World as Your Home — Being a Perpetual Traveler

Imagine traveling around the world during your retirement in a mobile home, remaining in a place for a few months, perhaps several months, enjoying the wonders of that stop, and then moving on to another. Not being a permanent resident or citizen of any country, you would not be liable for the payment of taxes.

This is not a new or radical idea; indeed people are already doing it. Depending upon the nature of their investments, they are maintaining their capital and much of the returns on their investments without being required to pay taxes.

These people use a large yacht as their mobile home and sail from place to place. Except for docking for weeks or months at destinations of their choice, they are perpetually traveling. When you are traveling, but are not a resident of a country — even if you visit for several months — you don't have to pay taxes in that country. Although countries vary in the length of time they permit visitors to stay tax-free (usually from three to nine months, depending on the country), this fact permits people to travel and reduce their taxes at the same time. Using the tax law of the United States offers a good example of the advantages of becoming a perpetual traveler during retirement. According to the U.S. Internal Revenue Service, a U.S. citizen, who is outside of the country for 330 days or more of a given tax year, is not liable for taxes on the first $70,000 earned outside of the country. An individual, therefore, who invests his or her assets in a country that has advantageous tax laws — some countries, for example, Andorra, Antigua, St. Kitts and Nevis, Anguilla, the

Residence Havens

Bahamas, and Cayman Islands, to list just some, have no income tax — can significantly reduce his or her tax burden. For some people it might even be possible to legally eliminate all taxes.

Your Yacht — An Oceanic Home

When someone says the word "yacht," many people think of a multi-million dollar vessel complete with full-time crew. In reality, large yachts capable of comfortable and safe ocean travel can be purchased new for under $200,000, the cost of a retirement home. A previously owned yacht in excellent condition can be purchased for less.

A sailboat of 65 feet easily accommodates a family comfortably for long voyages. These yachts are powered by both motor and sail, and can be equipped with all the conveniences of home — air-conditioning, dishwasher, clotheswasher and dryer, stove, microwave, TV and VCR. With the rapid expansion of the internet and satellite links for phones, you will find it easy to stay in touch in most of the well-traveled sea routes and ports.

Because banks treat yachts as homes, you can obtain a mortgage for a yacht. The interest payments on the mortgage are even tax-deductible, which is another advantage in offsetting any taxable income you might have.

A yacht's upkeep can be somewhat higher than the maintenance required for a house or condominium, but on the other hand, you'll be free from paying property taxes or condo maintenance fees. Overall, your upkeep costs should be about the same or less than the sum of the costs of upkeep and property taxes on a home. The newer the yacht you purchase, the fewer repairs will tend to be.

It's likely that the number of perpetual travelers will grow in places where destinations are close and countries welcome visitors. The Caribbean is one of these places. Some of the islands are within 25 miles of each other, and many permit visitors to stay three to nine months. Perpetual travelers can remain docked at a port until their time is up, then simply sail to another port. During their stays, they can use their yacht as their home base and explore and enjoy the island as they wish.

As the world becomes more modernized, and technological advances blur the lines between countries, citizenship and ties to the country of one's birth will become less important. If you choose to become a perpetual traveler, and the country in which you are currently a citizen enacts tax laws that are disadvantageous to your situation, you may simply renounce citizenship and become a citizen in a country that looks more favorably upon your situation.

For some people, especially those who like sailing and traveling, becoming a perpetual traveler during retirement is an option that promises truly unique and enjoyable golden years. For those who prefer a home on land, the countries and jurisdictions that follow offer a variety of opportunities and lifestyles.

The Principality of Andorra

Andorra is a small state, about 175 square miles (450 square kilometers) or half the size of New York City, located in the east Pyrenees Mountains. It is bordered by France on the north and Spain on the south.

Andorra is characterized by narrow valleys and mountain peaks that stretch for heights up to more than 8,850 feet (2,700 meters). Forests of birch and pine cover the mountains, below which are pastureland where sheep graze.

The population of Andorra is about 65,000, with 61% of its people being Spanish, 30% Andorran, and 6% French. Native Andorrans are Catalan in ancestry and language. Catalan is the official language of the principality, although French and Castillian are also widely spoken. Most Andorrans are Roman Catholics. The literacy rate of the principality is 99%, and its people enjoy quality health care. Andorra is a safe land with a low crime rate.

According to tradition, it is believed that Charlemagne declared Andorra to be a free state early in the 9th century. In 1278 Andorra came under the joint authority of the Count of Foix of France and the Catalan bishop of Urgel. Through the former, France's rights in the governing of the principality passed to the kings and chiefs of state of France. In March of 1993, Andorrans voted to end the system that had been in place for 715 years and adopt a parliamentary system of government.

Because of its small size and population, and its relative isolation, Andorra is not beset with the problems of larger countries. Even its capital city, Andorra la Vella, maintains the atmosphere of a small town.

Residence Havens

Despite its size, Andorra is a prosperous and modern land. The monetary unit of the principality is the French franc and the Spanish peseta. The economy centers around tourism, particularly skiing, although tobacco products are also important. Tourists are attracted to Andorra's slopes in winter, and its delightfully cool summer climate. A duty-free port, resulting in an active trading center, draws some 10 million tourists a year.

Possessing a modern infrastructure, Andorra is well positioned for continued economic prosperity. While the country has no airport or rail system, it has an excellent system of roadways. Its people have access to all the conveniences of the modern world.

Tax Facts of Interest

Along with its many attributes — its geography, strength of its economy, stability, and security — Andorra has no income taxes, making it a potentially excellent retirement haven.

For further information about Andorra, contact:

Andorran Mission to the United Nations
2 U.N. Plaza, 25th Floor
New York, NY 10018
Tel: 212-750-8064

There is also a private firm in Andorra which specializes in assisting prospective and current residents. They offer assistance with rental and purchase of apartments and homes, with residence permits, driver's licenses, car registration, mail handling in your absence, and many other things. I have spent many hours visiting with their managing director at their offices, and am impressed with the depth of knowledge of the country and the quality of their services. For more information contact:

Servissim
Edifici Areny, Baixos
Carretera General
Arinsal, La Massana
Principat d'Andorra
telephone: +376 837836
fax: +376 837179

Antigua and Barbuda

Antigua and Barbuda comprise an independent island country in the West Indies, in the eastern Caribbean Sea, east-southeast of Puerto Rico. The country consists of the islands of Antigua, Barbuda to its north, and Redonda, an uninhabited rocky islet to the southwest.

The country is small, about 170 square miles (440 square kilometers), about two and a half times the size of Washington, D.C. Most of Antigua is low-lying, but it does have a high point called Boggy Peak, which is about 1,330 feet (405 meters) in elevation. Barbuda is a flat, coral island that possesses exceptional beaches. The islands enjoy a tropical climate, however, because of local wind patterns suffer occasional droughts.

Antigua and Barbuda have a total population of about 66,000 people, comprised mostly of Africans, British, Portuguese, Lebanese, and Syrians. About 30% of the people live in an urban setting, with about 27,000 residing in the capital, St. John's. English is the country's official language, however, various local dialects are spoken. The major religions include Anglican, which is the predominate religion, other Protestant sects, and Roman Catholicism. The literacy rate is about 90%.

The islands offer a lifestyle typical of many of the islands of the Caribbean. A variety of activities and recreational pursuits are available; health care is considered to be good.

History and Government

In 1493 Christopher Columbus discovered and named Antigua. Because the island was inhabited by the fierce Carib Indians, the island was not permanently settled by Europeans until the British established an outpost in 1632. Settlers from Antigua settled Barbuda in 1661. Antigua remained closely tied to Great Britain until 1981, when it achieved independence as Antigua and Barbuda. However, the island government continues to maintain close ties to the United Kingdom, as well as the United States.

Citizens of the islands enjoy a government that is a parliamentary democracy, based on a constitution adopted on November 1, 1981. The country's legal system is based on English common law; suffrage is universal for those eighteen years of age and older. Although the chief of state is the queen, the monarchy is represented by a governor general. The actual head of the government is the prime minister, who carries out his duties with the help of the Council of Ministers. The Council is appointed by the governor general, on the advice of the prime minister, however. The country has a bicameral parliament, composed on a Senate and House of Representatives. A separate judicial branch of the government completes the government. Because of the historic close ties to the United Kingdom, Antigua and Barbuda enjoy a stable political and social system.

The Economy of Antigua and Barbuda

Like many islands of the Caribbean, tourism is a dominant economic activity, however, other sectors of the economy have gained in importance in recent years. Transportation, communications, general trade, and public utilities are sectors that have shown the greatest growth. The East Caribbean dollar is the monetary unit.

The infrastructure on the islands is solid. St. John's offers modern port facilities; the islands have paved roads, a railway system, and three airports. The telephone system is automated and has access to satellite communications.

Tax Facts of Interest

<u>Antigua and Barbuda do not tax personal income</u>. This is a major consideration for those retirees or investors who are interested in reducing or eliminating the taxes they must pay on income.

For further information on Antigua and Barbuda, contact the country's diplomatic representative in the United States:

Antigua and Barbuda
Chief of Mission
3216 New Mexico Ave., NW
Washington, D.C., 20016
Tel: 202-362-5211, 5166, 5122
Fax: 202-362-5225

Anguilla

Anguilla is a low-lying coral island located at the northern end of the Leeward Islands in the Caribbean Sea. It is a British dependency with internal self-government.

Being only 16 miles (25 kilometers) long and 3 miles (4.8 kilometers) wide, about 35 square miles (90 square kilometers) in total area, Anguilla is a small island. Its maximum elevation is about 200 feet (60 meters), and it possesses a tropical, semiarid climate.

With 12 miles (19 kilometers) of beautiful beaches Anguilla is a destination of tourists. A variety of activities, including swimming, boat racing, fishing, and snorkeling make it delightful place. While it may lack the cosmopolitan atmosphere of some of the other islands of the Caribbean, it more than makes up for this with a calmer, and to many, more enjoyable and peaceful lifestyle.

Anguilla has about 10,000 residents, the majority of whom are of African descent. English is the official language, and the capital is The Valley. Health care and education are good, a result of British administration over the years. Indeed, British influence can be found throughout the island.

History and Government

Anguilla's links to Britain date back to the colonial period. First discovered by Christopher Columbus in 1493, the island was not settled until 1650 when the British made it a colony. From the 18th century, the island was governed as a part of St. Kitts-Nevis-Anguilla. In 1967, however, rebellion and social unrest afflicted the island, culminating in 1969 with British intervention. Once

Residence Havens

order was restored, Anguilla became a British dependency with its own self-government. This arrangement was formalized in 1980 by the Anguilla Act. Today, Anguilla is a stable British dependent territory.

As a British dependency, the official head of state is the queen. However, actual administration of the island is managed through the office of the governor, who is the British monarch's representative, and an Executive Council consisting of the governor, the chief minister and not more than three other ministers. These ministers are appointed by the governor from elected members of the House of Assembly. The House of Assembly consists of seven members, elected for five-year terms, two ex-officio members, and two members nominated by the governor. The judicial system is based on the English system, with a final right of appeal to the Privy Council in the United Kingdom.

The Economy of Anguilla

While tourism is a major part of the island's economy, many residents are occupied with fishing and subsistence farming. There is little manufacturing or industry on the island. On the whole, the island's infrastructure is sound, designed and maintained by the British. Islanders use both the Eastern Caribbean dollar and the U.S. dollar for currency.

Tax Facts of Interest

Anguilla has few taxes. <u>The island has no income taxes, no corporate taxes, no sales taxes, no value added taxes, no capital gains taxes, no interest taxes, nor any of the hosts of minor taxes many other governments include in their tax codes.</u> The tax code of Anguilla clearly encourages investment.

The island does, of course, need to raise revenue to operate the government. It does this through taxes on hotels — paid by tourists — taxes on imports, the sale of land to foreigners, and a lottery. These sources (along with British aid) have been sufficient to maintain the duties and obligations of the government.

Although Anguilla, because of its size and population, lacks the luster of some of the other Caribbean islands, it is a rather delightful place. Certainly, its tax code is one of the most advantageous of any.

For further information on Anguilla, contact:

Anguilla Tourist Board
World Trade Centre
Suite 250
San Francisco, CA 94111
Tel: 415-398-3231
Fax: 415-398-3669

Anguilla Tourist Board
P.O. Box 1388
The Valley
Anguilla
Tel: 809-497-2759
Toll Free: 800-553-4939
Fax: 809-497-2710

Anguilla Tourist Board
Windotel
3 Epirus Road
London SW6 7UJ
Tel: 011-441-71-937-7725
Fax: 011-441-71-938-4793

Argentina

Argentina is a large country, roughly triangular in shape and covering much of the southern part of South America. From north to south, the country extends slightly over 2,000 miles (3,300 kilometers), and from east to west a little more than 850 miles (1,380 kilometers), giving it a total area of 1,068,120 square miles (2,766,889 square kilometers). The country has 1,656 miles (2,665 kilometers) of coastline.

Being such a large country, Argentina possesses a diverse topography with a mix of mountains, highlands, and vast plains. Many mountain peaks surpass 12,000 feet (3,660 meters), with Aconcagua at 22,831 feet (6,959 meters) being the tallest mountain in the Western Hemisphere. In the north Argentina has vast forested flatlands called the Chaco, south of which is the Pampas, an expanse of treeless plains that includes much of the country's great agricultural areas.

Although Argentina lies in the temperate zone, its climate varies with latitude and elevation. In Buenos Aires, the nation's capital, for example, the average July temperature is 74 degrees F (23 degrees C), and the average winter temperature is 49 degrees F (9.5 degrees C). Precipitation likewise varies, depending upon local conditions, however, it tends to be higher in the north and lower in the south. The average annual rainfall around Buenos Aires is about 40 inches (100 centimeters).

Argentina has about 34,000,000 people, with about 85% of them living in or close to urban centers. Close to a third of the country's population resides in or near Buenos Aires. Eight out of ten Argentineans are of European descent, mostly Spanish and Italian with smaller percentages of French, British, German, Polish, and Russian. Mestizos and native Indians comprise a fraction of the overall percentage of the population.

Spanish heritage is found throughout the country. The official language of the nation is Spanish, and 90% of the people are Roman Catholics. Protestants, Jews, and some non-Christian religions are also represented.

Argentina, which once was considered to be a third-world country, has modernized rapidly. Its health care has high standards (especially in the major cities), its literacy rate is 95%, and education is highly valued. Argentineans enjoy a modern lifestyle.

History and Government

The Spanish navigator Juan Diaz de Solis, while searching for a southwest passage to the Indies in 1516, sailed into the Rio de la Plata and claimed the land around it for Spain. This land came to be known as Argentina. The first permanent settlement was established by 1553, and by the 1580s Spain was in firm control, remaining in control until 1816 when Argentina declared itself free. It wasn't until 1853, however, that a federal constitution was adopted. This constitution was modeled on the Constitution of the United States.

Today, Argentina is a federal republic. The chief of state is the president, who performs his duties with the aid of a council of ministers. A national congress and judicial system complete the government. Argentineans, 18 years and older, possess the right to vote.

The Economy of Argentina

During the nineties, Argentina has built a solid economy, positioning itself for growth of high potential. The country has abundant resources, including superior farmland, minerals, natural gas, and petroleum, which are being developed and helping to sustain growth. Manufacturing has also expanded rapidly, as has the service sector, particularly tourism.

Argentina

Throughout much of this century, Argentina's infrastructure lagged behind the needs of the country. Today, the government is addressing those needs through a significant modernization program in transportation and telecommunications.

Argentina's monetary unit is the peso. The country's financial system has become responsive to the needs of business, investors, and consumers, helping to ensure Argentina's economy.

Tax Facts of Interest

Argentina does not tax income from foreign sources. In addition, authors and book publishers enjoy exemptions from income tax.

Although the government does not offer some of the tax incentives that other places do, Argentina's rich Spanish heritage provides the country with a unique identity, which newcomers often find enthralling. The country possesses a rich culture in literature, art, and music, along with spectacular natural geography. Buenos Aires is a city that offers beauty and history, as well as the conveniences and pleasures of modern life.

Should you wish to find out more information about Argentina, contact:

The Embassy of Argentina
1600 New Hampshire Ave., NW
Washington, DC 20009
Tel: 202-939-6400

Aruba

Aruba is an island of the Lesser Antilles, located in the Caribbean Sea near Venezuela. The island belongs to the Netherlands and is administered as the Netherlands Antilles. Aruba is a rather small island, about 19 miles long (30 kilometers) and 5 miles wide (8 kilometers) with a total area of about 75 square miles (193 square kilometers).

Aruba's climate is delightful and nearly constant. Throughout the year temperatures average between 85 and 95 degrees F (29 and 35 degrees C) during the day and 75 to 85 degrees F (24 and 29 degrees C) at night. The tradewinds blow consistently between 10 and 20 mph (16 and 32 kph). Aruba does not have a rainy season; occasional showers, usually of short duration occur from mid October to November. Although showers do occur during other months, they are less frequent.

Slightly over 67,000 people live year-round in Aruba. Most speak Dutch, the official language, although English, Spanish, and Papiamento, a mixture of mostly Dutch, English, Spanish and Portuguese, are widely spoken. The ethnic breakdown of the population is mixed European and Caribbean Indians (which make up about 80% of Aruba's people). Roman Catholicism is the predominate religion, with Protestants making up about 8% of the religious population with smaller percentages of Hindus, Muslims, and Jews. The island's health care and educational systems are of high quality. The principal town, Oranjestad, located at the west end of the island, is also the capital city.

Aruba offers a variety of wonderful activities. Watersports, snorkling, diving, horseback riding, excellent nightclubs, fine restaurants, shows, and gambling are just some pursuits of interest. Of course, the beaches, spectacular

25

climate, and tropical environment also help to make Aruba an outstanding destination.

History and Government

In 1499, the Spanish explorer Alonso de Ojeda sighted the island and claimed it for Spain. Because the island had no gold, silver, or other precious metals, and was too arid for large-scale farming, the Spanish made little use of it.

It wasn't until 1636 that Aruba became important to the Europeans, and it was the Dutch, not the Spanish who had the greatest interest. Seeking to establish a colonial presence in the Caribbean, the Dutch captured several islands from the Spanish, one of which was Aruba. Except for a short time during the Napoleonic Wars, Aruba has remained under Dutch control. During that time the Dutch have bestowed

much of their culture and political institutions throughout the region. Today, Aruba is filled with examples of Dutch influence from language and architecture to a unique blend of Dutch and Indian culture.

For many years administered by the Dutch, Aruba has evolved as a stable, self-ruling society. Its laws are based on the Dutch civil system with some influence from English common law.

Aruba enjoys full autonomy in internal affairs while remaining a part of the Dutch realm. The island was scheduled to gain full independence in 1996, but it requested and received cancellation of the agreement, prefering to remain as part of the Netherlands.

The chief of state is the monarch of the Netherlands, who is represented by a governor. The head of government is the prime minister who shares power with a unicameral legislature. A judicial branch completes the government. Suffrage is universal for individuals 18 years of age and older.

The Economy of Aruba

While tourism is the mainstain of Aruba's economy, oil refining, offshore banking, and storage facilities are also important. Aruba enjoys a strong economy with an unemployment rate of less than 1%. The island is a major tourist attraction. Modern hotels dot its marvelous beaches, and countless small shops are found in its towns. The refining of crude oil is another important sector of the economy, providing the island with significant revenue and employment, while offshore banking and storage are fast-growing sectors.

While Aruba has its own currency — the Aruban florin — U.S. dollars are accepted virtually everywhere. Currencies from other countries are easily exchanged at banks, and major credit cards are also accepted.

Being a major tourist site, the Aruban government is aware of the importance of a sound infrastructure. The island has two airports, three seaports, and excellent telecommunications networks.

Tax Facts of Interest

Aruba offers a low tax rate for wealthy foreign residents. If you wish to obtain a residency permit, which is required after 90 days, you will be expected to demonstrate the financial resources necessary to support yourself and your family without working. Although Aruba does not offer some of the tax incentives other retirement havens do, its truly outstanding environment makes it an exceptional place to live.

Should you wish to find out more information about Aruba, contact:

Aruba Tourism Authority
L.G. Smith Blvd. 172
Aruba, Dutch Carribean
Tel: 2978-21019 or 23778 (P.R. Dept.)
Fax: 2978-34702 or 30075 (P.R. Dept.)

Aruba Tourism Authority
2344 Salzedo St.
Miami, FL 33144-5033
Tel: 305-567-2720
Fax: 305-567-2721

Aruba Tourism Authority
1000 Harbor Blvd.
Weehawken, NJ 07087
Tel: 201-330-0800 or 800-TOARUBA
Fax: 201-330-8757

Aruba Tourism Authority
Schimmelpennincncklann 1
2517 JN — The Hague
The Netherlands
Tel: 70-356-6220
Fax: 70-360-4877

The Bahamas

Most people don't realize that The Bahamas are a large group of islands. Thirty inhabited islands and thousands of uninhabited islets and cays stretch over thousands of square miles starting 50 miles (80 kilometers) off the Florida coast. For many, The Bahamas are a place of wonder and variety. Miles of astonishing shoreline with some of the world's most beautiful beaches, cosmopolitan Nassau, and islands dotted with villages set against a backdrop of palms make The Bahamas a unique place.

The Bahamas begin off the coast of Florida and extend over 100,000 square miles (260,000 square kilometers) of the Atlantic to roughly 60 miles (96 kilometers) off Cuba. The total land area is 5,400 square miles (13,900 square kilometers). The climate is one of year-round summer. The average high temperature is 80 degrees F (27 degrees C) and the average low is 70 degrees F (21 degrees C) from spring through fall. In the winter, night time temperatures might fall to about 60 degrees F (16 C). Sunshine is abundant; showers, when they come, usually arrive in the early morning or late afternoon and are of short duration.

The population of the The Bahamas is about 273,000 people, with blacks comprising about 85% and white (British, Canadian, and U.S.) making up the rest. The principal languages are English and Creole. About 32% of the population are Baptists, 20% are Anglicans, and 19% are Roman Catholics. Other Protestant sects are also represented. The general population is educated — the literacy rate is 98% — and enjoys fine health care.

Although the islands of The Bahamas are diverse, each having its own individual characteristics, the islands share a unique charm that has made them a favorite destination of people the world over. Countless activities, from watersports to quiet beaches to history, culture, and a nightlife (especially on Nassau) second to none make the islands a delightful place to visit and live in.

History and Government

It is believed that Christopher Columbus first set foot on San Salvador in 1492. No one knows exactly where he came ashore, however, and four separate monuments presumably mark the spot. When Columbus saw the Arawak Indians who inhabited the island — which is only 63 square miles (163 square kilometers) in area — he assumed he had reached India and called them Indians. Throughout the Age of European Exploration, many of the islands of The Bahamas were visited, but it was not until 1647 that the British began settlement. In 1783 the islands became a British colony, and remained such until 1964 when internal self-government was granted. The Bahamas attained full independence within the Commonwealth in 1973.

Because of the long association with Great Britain, the islands exhibit much English influence. They have also enjoyed remarkable stability.

The government of The Bahamas is a commonwealth. The capital city is Nassau. The chief of state is the British monarch, who appoints and is represented by the governor general. The actual head of the government is the prime minister, who is appointed by the governor general. The legislature is a bicameral parliament comprised of the Senate, whose members are appointed by the governor general, and the House of Assembly, whose members are elected by the people. Suffrage is universal, starting at 18 years of age. The judicial system is based on English common law.

Economy of The Bahamas

With its islands approaching paradise in beauty and splendor, tourism is quite naturally the mainstain of The Bahamas' economy. Indeed tourism accounts for close to 50% of the islands' GDP. Banking, pharmaceuticals, and the production of rum are other important economic activities.

Of the many islands in the Western Hemisphere, The Bahamas have one of the most up-to-date infrastructures. Air- and seaports have modern equipment, roads are well maintained, and telecommunications are state-of-the-art. In every area, The Bahamas can accommodate the needs of virtually every resident and visitor. Unquestionably, the islands are a marvelous place to live.

Tax Facts of Interest

The Bahamas offer a variety of tax advantages. <u>There is no income tax, no death duties in respect of real or personal estates, no succession, estate, or inheritance taxes, no income taxes on companies, no dividend taxes, and no gift taxes</u>.

The Bahamas' chief source of income is derived from import duties.

Should you wish to find out more information about The Bahamas, you may contact:

The Bahamas Tourism Office
2957 Clairmont Rd., Suite 150
Atlanta, GA 30329
Tel: 404-633-1793
Fax: 404-633-1575

Residence Havens

The Bahamas Tourism Office
150 E. 52nd St.
28th Floor North
New York, NY 10022
Tel: 212-758-2777
Fax: 212-753-6531

The Bahamas Tourism Office
3, The Billings
Walnut Tree Close
Guilford, Surrey GUI 4UL
England
Tel: 01483-448900
Fax: 01483-448990

The Bahamas Tourism Office
P.O. Box N 3701
Nassau, The Bahamas
Tel: 242-322-7500
Fax: 242-328-0945

Embassy of The Bahamas
2220 Massachusetts Ave., NW
Washington, DC 20008
Tel: 202-319-2660
Fax: 202-319-2668

Bermuda

Bermuda, often thought of as a single island, is actually a group of islands in the North Atlantic Ocean, east of North Carolina. Although about 150 islands comprise the Bermuda group, only about 20 are inhabited and only six are important. The "Bermuda" people usually refer to is called the Main Island and also Great Bermuda. This island is about 14 miles long (23 kilometers). The total area of the island group is about 20 square miles (53 square kilometers). This is about 30% the size of Washington, D.C. Bermuda is a dependent territory of the United Kingdom, enjoying the benefits of that status.

The islands have an interesting foundation, their base being of volcanic rock capped with coral formations. On the north, west, and south they are enclosed by reefs, most of which are submerged. The islands are connected by narrow channels. Generally low-lying, the islands are hilly but rise only about 260 feet (80 meters) above sea level.

Bermuda enjoys a subtropical climate. It is mild and humid. In summer the temperature averages about 70 degrees F (21 degrees C), while in winter temperatures average near 63 degrees F (17 degrees C). Lying within the Gulf Stream, southern winds bring humidity, which results in yearly rainfall of about 58 inches (1470 centimeters) per year. Nevertheless, the overall climate includes plenty of sunshine.

This sunshine and rainfall, coupled with the warm moist air, supports luxuriant vegetation, giving Bermuda a picturesque setting. Numerous flowering plants, bamboo, palm, and mangrove thickets are characteristic of the islands. Of course, all this makes Bermuda a tourist and vacation site.

Approximately 62,000 people live on the Bermuda islands. About 60% of the population is black, and the rest is mostly white. Slightly more than 35% of the people are affiliated with the Anglican church, about 15% are Roman Catholics, 10% are African Methodist Episcopal, 6% are Methodists, with the rest of the church-going population adhering to a variety of faiths. English is the predominate language, and the literacy rate is 98%. Health care is very good.

History and Government

Bermuda was discovered by a Spanish navigator, Juan de Bermudez, who was shipwrecked there about 1503. Although the islands are named after him, it wasn't until 1609 that the first settlement was founded. This settlement was in fact an accident when Sir George Somers and a party of English colonists, who had originally set sail for Virginia, and like de Bermudez a hundred years earlier, became shipwrecked. In 1612 "Somers Islands" were included in the third charter of the Virginia Company, and a second group of British colonists arrived. In 1684 the original charter was revoked and the islands became a crown colony. In time, they also were referred to more as Bermuda than as Somers Islands. Bermuda became internally self-governing in 1968.

Today, Bermuda remains a dependant territory of the United Kingdom, with its capital at Hamilton. The chief of state is the British monarch, who appoints the islands' governor to represent the crown. The head of government is the premier, who is appointed by the governor, who is turn nominates a cabinet that is also appointed by the governor. Bermuda's legislative branch consists of a bicameral parliament. The members of the Senate are appointed by the governor, however the members of the House of Assembly are elected by citizens 18 years or age and older. The judicial system is based on English common law, embodied in a constitution.

Bermuda's Economy

One of the highest per capital incomes in the world is found in Bermuda. Its GDP per capita is $28,000 (based on the recent estimates). Having taken advantage of its prime location, Bermuda enjoys a thriving tourist industry, with over 90% of its business coming from North America. The industrial sector is small, as is agriculture due to a lack of land suitable for farming. Nevertheless, Bermuda does enjoy several other sectors that support its economy, including finance, pharmaceuticals, ship repairing, structural concrete products, and paints.

With an economy built around tourism, Bermuda's officials have always striven to maintain a modern infrastructure. Its airport and seaport are modern in their capacity and equipment, its roadways are more than adequate, and its telecommunication system is fully automatic. Its international links include submarine cables as well as satellite communications.

The islands' currency is the Bermudian dollar, which equals the U.S. dollar. This value is a fixed rate.

Tax Facts of Interest

Bermuda is a wonderful place to live, however, it is expensive. <u>There is no income tax in Bermuda</u>, but it is extremely difficult to obtain a residency permit. Usually, a resident must buy property costing at least a million dollars.

Residence Havens

While Bermuda, because of its potentially high costs, may not be everyone's retirement haven, those who can afford it may indeed find that they have discovered a unique and ideal place to spend their retirement years.

Should you like to find out more information about Bermuda, contact the following:

Bermuda Tourism Office
Global House
43 Church St.
Hamilton HM 11
Bermuda
Tel: 441-292-0023
Fax: 441-292-7537

Bermuda Department of Tourism
245 Peachtree Center Avenue, NE
Suite 803
Atlanta, GA   30303
Tel: 404-524-1541

Bermuda Department of Tourism
310 Madison Ave., Suite 201
New York, NY 10017
Tel: 212-818-9800 or 800-223-6106 or 800-BERMUDA

Bermuda Department of Tourism
1200 Bay St., Suite 1004
Toronto M5R 2A5
Canada
Tel: 416-923-9600

Bermuda Department of Tourism
1 Battersea Church Rd.
London, SW11 3LY
England
Tel: 171-743-8813

Bermuda

*Bermuda Department of Tourism
Herzogspitalstrasse 5 80331
Munich
Germany
Tel: 011-49-892-67874*

Bolivia

Bolivia is a republic in central South America. It is a landlocked country, bordered on the north and east by Brazil, on the southeast by Paraguay, on the south by Argentina, and on the west by Chile and Peru. A large country, Boliva is about 424,000 square miles (1,098,500 square kilometers) in area.

Bolivia is a land of contrasts, possessing mountains, expansive plains, plateaus, and lowlands. The great central plateau, averaging an altitude of 12,000 feet (3,600 meters), lies between two great cordilleras that have three of the highest peaks in South America. Lake Titicaca, on the Peruvian border, is the highest lake in the world at 12,056 feet (3,616 meters). In the east central part of the country, semitropical forests dominate the landscape, while in the east are Amazon-Chaco lowlands.

Because it is a land of varied elevation, Bolivia, despite being located in the tropical zone, has a wide range of climates. In the higher regions, the climate varies from temperate to cold, while in the low-lying regions, the climate is warmer. The country's average temperatures range from about 47 degrees F (8 degrees C) in the upland plateau regions to about 80 degrees F (26 degrees C) in the lowlands. Like the temperature, the country's rainfall varies by region. Overall, however, Bolivia's climate is considered to be a rather pleasant one.

Bolivia has slightly over 7,100,000 people. Although Bolivia was once a Spanish colony, and much Spanish heritage is evident, the country also possesses a large native Indian population. Thus, Spanish, Quechua, and Aymara are all official languages. While Spanish is the preferred language of government and business, it is estimated that up to 40% of the Indian population does not speak Spanish. The country's ethnic divisions include Quechua,

30%, Aymara, 25%, Mestizo (mixed European and Indian ancestry), 25%-30%, and European, 5%-15%. About 95% of Bolivia's are Roman Catholics, with a small portion being Protestant.

Bolivia is a country that is lagging behind many of its South American neighbors in education and health care. About 80% of the population is literate, although this percentage drops as one goes into the smaller, more isolated villages. Health care, while of good quality in the major cities, decreases in quality the farther from the cities and principal towns one travels. The quality of health care is clearly reflected in the nation's life expectancy rates: 57 years for men and 63 years for women, numbers that are well below those of advanced countries.

History and Government

Bolivia's recorded history begins with the Incas in the 13th century, who conquered the region from the earlier Indian inhabitants. The Spanish gained control of the land in the 1530s and remained in control until 1825 when Bolivia (named after Simon Bolivar, the South American independence fighter) won its independence.

Unfortunately, Bolivia has not enjoyed stability throughout its history. Not only has the country suffered wars with Chile and Brazil, it has experienced much domestic turmoil. During the last several years, however, the government has made attempts to insure a stable political and economic climate.

Today Bolivia is a republic, with the seat of government located at La Paz. The head of the government is the president, who is elected for a four-year term. Suffrage is universal and compulsory for married individuals of 18, and 21 for unmarried citizens. The legislature is composed of a bicameral national congress, while its judiciary is based on a constitution adopted in 1967.

Bolivia's Economy

Bolivia is generally acknowledged to be one of the poorest and least developed of the countries of Latin America. However, the country has in recent years experienced generally improving economic conditions. Realizing that the country has fallen behind many of its neighbors, the government has taken steps to maintain fiscal discipline (which has reduced inflation and kept it in check), and just as importantly initiated and continued free-market policies. Privatization has been a serious goal, which has seen success with the electric power generation sector, the state airline, state telephone, and the national railroad all being privatized.

Unquestionably, Bolivia has enormous pent up demand for countless products. This demand represents a potentially major market, which in turn could portend significant and steady economic growth. The country's currency is based on the boliviano.

Being one of the continent's poorest nations, Bolivia's infrastructure is lacking in many important areas. Overall, its roads, airports, and telecommunications systems need to be updated. Modernization, of course, is happening faster in the major cities than in the countryside.

Tax Facts of Interest

Bolivia has an assortment of taxes. Indeed, there are few regulations of which taxpayers may take advantage. However, in an effort to stimulate the country's economy, Bolivia has created Free Zones.

These Free Zones offer investors potentially significant advantages. Nationals or foreigners may be authorized to operate an enterprise in a Free Zone. Operations in a Free Zone may be industrial, commercial, or

Residence Havens

warehousing in nature. <u>Investments in Free Zones are exempted from most Bolivian taxes</u>.

For the retiree who wishes to invest his or her funds in this type of environment, Bolivia may be the perfect situation. However, Bolivia, as a retirement haven, is likely to appeal only to those individuals who are looking for a unique investment situation along with retirement.

Should you wish to find out more information about Bolivia, contact:

The Bolivian Embassy
3014 Massachusetts Ave., NW
Washington, DC 20008
Tel: 202-483-4410 through 4412
Fax: 202-328-3712

Campione

Campione is a very small area of Italy that is completely surrounded by Switzerland. Located on the shores of Lake Lugano, Campione, although part of Italy and subject to Italian laws, functions much as a part of Switzerland. The enclave uses Swiss facilities such as the post office, telecommunications services, and banks. Even cars carry Swiss license plates.

Located in the Swiss Canton of Ticino, Campione is about 16 miles from the Italian border. It is, in many ways, a very unique place. Perhaps of most importance to people considering a new residence is that there are no border controls, permitting easy access in and out of Campione. This access includes Switzerland and Liechtenstein. Together with attractive tax laws, this access makes Campione extremely attractive as a residence site.

Campione's climate is much like that of Switzerland's: generally temperate (except on the highest elevations). The average annual average temperature is about 50 degrees F (10 degrees C), and yearly rainfall is moderate, coming mostly in the winter in the form of snow. Overall, the climate is not severe.

The population of the enclave is about 2,000, mostly Italian combined with a mix of Swiss and other ethnic Europeans. The official language of the enclave is Italian.

Campione offers a high quality style of life with plenty of activities, including skiing, water sports, and golf. The Italian city of Milan with its marvelous cultural attractions is but an hour away, while many of the delightful attractions of Switzerland are even closer.

History and Government

Campione can trace its status back to the 13th century when the Lord of Campione presented the village of Campione and its territory to the Church of St. Ambrosius of Milan. Not until the end of the 18th century did this arrangement end with Campione joining the Cisalpine Republic. Not long afterward, Austria gained control of Campione, after which the enclave was incorporated into the Kingdom of Italy.

Although Campione is a part of Italy, being surrounded by Switzerland makes the enclave unique. The enclave is subject to Italian law, however, its residents enjoy special benefits, particularly regarding taxation.

The Economy of Campione

Campione's economy is built around a municipal casino and other recreational activities. Obviously, because of its small size, its economy is not large. Nevertheless, the residents of the enclave must be judged prosperous.

Tax Facts of Interest

Campione's tax laws are of special interest to those seeking a fine retirement haven. The enclave enjoys special tax advantages. <u>There is no personal income tax and no municipal tax. Furthermore, residents of Campione are not subject to Switzerland's double taxation agreements with other nations, including most of western Europe, the U.S., and Canada.</u>

Should you wish to find out more information about Campione, you will likely need to visit the enclave yourself. Unfortunately, the enclave does little promotion of its unusual and advantageous status, and there is no source for definitive information. No promotional literature or brochures are currently available.

Your best approach for determining if Campione is a suitable retirement haven is to visit the enclave and get to know it and its people.

The Cayman Islands

The Cayman Islands, a dependency of Great Britain, are located in the Caribbean Sea. Three islands comprise the group: Grand Cayman, which lies northwest of Jamaica, Little Cayman and Cayman Brac, about 80 miles (130 kilometers) northeast of Grand Cayman. For general location, the Cayman Islands are about halfway between Cuba and Honduras.

The islands, which are low-lying and of coral formation, are small with a total area of about 100 square miles (260 square kilometers). Their total land area is about 1.5 times the size of Washington, D.C. The highest point of the islands is the Bluff, about 142 feet (43 meters). Enjoying a tropical marine climate, with warm rainy summers and cool, relatively dry winters, and endowed with fine beaches, tourism is an important industry to the Cayman Islands.

Close to 35,000 people live on the islands. About 40% are of mixed race, 20% are white, 20% are black, and 20% are of various ethnic groups. Residents are most likely to belong to one of the following churches: Anglican, Baptist, Roman Catholic, Presbyterian, or Church of God. Other Protestant denominations are also represented.

Because the islands are a dependency of Great Britain, the British have maintained an excellent infrastructure. Education on the Cayman Islands is good, with a literacy rate of 98%, and health care is of high quality.

Along with their excellent climate, the Cayman Islands offer a variety of activities and pastimes. Fine dining and entertainment, fishing, shopping, boating, swimming, and snorkeling are just some recreational pursuits available to visitors and island dwellers. The Cayman Islands are an excellent retirement haven.

History and Government

Christopher Columbus first sighted the Cayman Islands in 1503, naming them Las Tortugas, Spanish for "turtles." Spain showed little interest in the islands, however, and they were not colonized until 1734 by British settlers who came from Jamaica. The islands remained a British dependency until 1959 when they became a self-governing member of the Federation of the West Indies, but then decided to become a British dependency again in 1962, which they are yet today.

Based on British common law and local statues, the constitution of the Cayman Islands was first written in 1959 and revised in 1972 and 1992. The chief of state is the British monarch, while the head of government is the governor and president of the Executive Council. A cabinet consists of three members appointed by the governor and four members elected by the Legislative Assembly. The legislative branch of the government is a unicameral assembly; suffrage is universal for citizens 18 years of age and older. The Cayman Islands have no formal political parties and are stable and secure.

The Economy of the Cayman Islands

Citizens of the Cayman Islands enjoy one of the highest standards of living in the world. Tourism — close to a million tourists a year visit the islands — and an offshore financial center are the mainstays of the economy, with fishing, shipbuilding, construction, turtle raising, and farming being important to some locales. The currency of the islands is the Caymanian dollar.

Residents of the islands benefit from a solid infrastructure. Two seaports and three airports provide easy access to the islands, while a modern phone system, including satellite links, supports efficient communication.

Tax Facts of Interest

Residents of the Cayman Islands benefit from <u>no direct taxation. There is no income tax</u>.

The Cayman Islands have an established government policy to encourage newcomers of good repute and financial standing to seek permanent resident status. In general, an applicant for residency must be in a financial position to support him- or herself and dependents and must be able to invest in a home or local business. This investment must be at least an equivalent of U.S. $180,000. To facilitate residency applications, the islands have set up an office applicants may contact. Applications may be sent to:

The Chief Immigration Officer
Department of Immigration
P.O. Box 1098
Grand Cayman, BWI

Should you wish to find out more about the Cayman Islands, contact any of the offices of the Cayman Islands Department of Tourism:

Department of Tourism
P.O. Box 67, George Town
Grand Cayman, BWI
Tel: 345-949-0623
Fax: 345-949-4053

Department of Tourism
6100 Blue Lagoon Drive, Suite 150
Miami, FL 33126-2085
Tel: 305-266-2300
Fax: 305-267-2932

Residence Havens

*Department of Tourism
420 Lexington Ave., Suite 2733
New York, NY 10170
Tel: 212-682-5582
Fax: 212-986-5123*

*Department of Tourism
6 Arlington St.
London, SW1A 1RE
England, United Kingdom
Tel: 0171-491-7771
Fax: 0171-409-7773*

*International Travel Produce, Inc.
Kawase Building, 4th Floor
14-1, 2 Chome
Tsukui Chuo-ku, Tokyo 104
Tel: 03-3545-6187
Fax: 03-3545-8756*

Ceuta and Melilla

Ceuta and Melilla are two small enclaves on the coast of Morocco. Despite seemingly being a part of Morocco, they actually belong to Spain. For a variety of factors, including their pleasant climate, duty-free ports, strong economies, modern facilities, and beneficial tax laws, both are potentially superior retirement havens.

Ceuta is a city and seaport in northwest Africa, located on the Strait of Gibraltar. Bordered by Morocco, the city is an enclave of Spain and is governed as part of Ca diz province in Spain. Ceuta is situated on the site of ancient Abila, which is thought by scholars to be one of the two Pillars of Hercules. Positioned on a headland consisting of seven peaks, the city lies at the end of a narrow isthmus. Its total area is about nine square miles (about 23 square kilometers).

Melilla is located slightly more than 150 nautical miles east of Ceuta and stands on a large cape which extends some 15 miles out from the coast. The area of Melilla is about 4 square miles (about 10 square kilometers). Melilla is administered by the Spanish province of Malaga.

The cities enjoy a mild Mediterranean subtropical climate. Winter is the rainy season while summer tends to be dry.

Ceuta and Melilla have about 80,000 residents each. Close to 80% of the residents are Spanish, with much of the rest being Moroccan. Residents of Indian descent comprise about 1% of the population. Most of the Spanish residents adhere to the Roman Catholic faith while most of the Moroccans are Muslim. Both Spanish and Moroccan are widely spoken, however, Spanish is the predominate language of business and government.

Residence Havens

Because both cities have excellent seaports — though Ceuta's port is built around a natural harbor and is larger than Melilla's — recreational pleasure craft that ply the Mediterranean call the ports home. Ceuta's port, especially, is often filled with pleasure craft.

History and Government

Ceuta and Melilla have a long history. Both cities date their original establishment to the Phoenicians, the sailors and merchants of the ancient Mediterranean.

Ceuta later became the site of a Carthaginian settlement, which was taken over eventually by the Romans. In the 5th century the city was captured by the Vandals, who in time lost it to Byzantium. After that the Visigoths, Arabs, Portuguese, and finally the Spanish in 1580 seized control. Since that time, except for a period from 1694 to 1720 when the Moors gained control, the enclave has remained a jurisdiction of Spain.

Melilla's history is quite similar. It, too, was established by the Phoenicians, and subsequently was ruled by the Carthaginians, Romans, Byzantines, and various Berber dynasties until it was conquered by Spain in 1497.

Today, the cities have their own civil governments. Although they are officially considered to be a part of Spanish provinces, they enjoy a somewhat unique status. Each city has one deputy and two senators in the Spanish Parliament. Moreover, the provincial governments provide little actual governmental functions; the local administration of each city largely carries out the tasks of government. Ceuta and Melilla are, in a practical sense, separated from Spain by the Mediterranean Sea but also by their local administrations.

If there is a long-term concern over the stability of Ceuta and Melilla, it is that Morocco would like to negotiate control of the enclaves. However, Spain has little intention of giving up what it considers to be part of its territory and it appears that the status quo will remain.

The Economies of Ceuta and Melilla

While Melilla is smaller than Ceuta, and has a smaller port, these enclaves are both modern and prosperous. Because of its smaller size, smaller port, and the fact that its location does not allow it to take advantage of the sea traffic that plies the strait, Melilla is the less cosmopolitan of the two enclaves.

Ceuta, on the other hand, has a fine natural harbor, and its port is far busier than most of the ports of mainland Spain. The enclave's location at the busy strait gives it an advantage most cities envy. In addition, Ceuta is only an hour away from Algeciras, Spain by ferry. Because this is a shorter route than Tangiers, Morocco to Algeciras, Ceuta, for many, provides easier entry to Spain. Also important is Ceuta's designation as a duty-free port of entry for Spain. This designation has led to the proliferation of numerous shops selling countless items. Of course, all this results in a healthy, vigorous economy.

The easy access of each of the enclaves to Spain and the rest of Europe, their pleasant climate, and prosperity make Ceuta and Melilla attractive sites for those considering retirement, as well as those contemplating the establishment of a business.

Tax Facts of Interest

Ceuta and Melilla both have appealing tax structures. Because the cities are Spanish, <u>Spain's tax system applies, however, the taxes apply at only half the rate one would pay in Spain. Furthermore, residents of the enclaves enjoy the benefits of all Spanish double taxation treaties</u>. It is also noteworthy that the enclaves are duty-free ports, <u>there is no VAT (value added tax)</u>, and the cost of maintaining a residence is quite low compared to other retirement havens.

Should you like to find out additional information about Ceuta and Melilla, contact:

The Embassy of Spain
2375 Pennsylvania Ave., NW
Washington, D.C. 20037
Tel: 202-452-0100, 728-2340
Fax: 202-833-5670

Costa Rica

Costa Rica is the most democratic and stable country in Central America. Compared to other Latin American countries, it has few extremes of wealth and poverty, has no standing army, and is the site of some of the most spectacular nature in the world. Drawn by the delightful environment and financial incentives, close to 30,000 U.S. citizens have moved to the country in recent years.

Bordered by Nicaragua on the north and Panama on the south, Costa Rica has a total area of 19,730 square miles (about 51,000 square kilometers) and is slightly smaller than the state of West Virginia. Its land is comprised of coastal lowlands and an interior plateau with altitudes of about 4,000 feet (1,200 meters). The country also contains rugged mountains, its highest point being Cerro Chirripo at nearly 12,200 feet (3,810 meters).

The climate of Costa Rica is tropical, with a dry season that runs from December to April and a rainy season from May to November. Temperatures vary with altitude. The lowlands, of course, are much hotter than the plateau and mountainous regions. The average temperature for the central and mountain valley areas is 68 degrees F (20 degrees C) and 79 degrees (26 degrees C) for the low-lying coastal lands.

In recent years, Costa Rica has appeared in various publications and news reports as a retirement haven. In many respects, these articles and reports are true. The country clearly offers many benefits to individuals seeking retirement in a tropical land that provides a refreshing lifestyle.

About 3,500,000 people live in Costa Rica. Whites (including Mestizos) make up close to 96% of the country's population with blacks, 2%, Indians, 1%, and Chinese, 1%, comprising the rest. The official language of the country is Spanish, although English is common around Puerto Limon. By far the predominate religion is Roman Catholic with about 95% of Costa Ricans belonging to this faith.

Costa Rica is, without argument, one of the most advanced countries in Latin America. It has a high quality system of health care, which is apparent from life expectancy rates: 76 years for males and 80 years for females. The country has one physician for every 980 people. Travelers are advised, however, that the quality and availability of health care diminish as one moves away from main cities. Education also has a high priority in Costa Rica, with the literacy rate being 95%. Both health care and education are most advanced in and around major population areas.

Residents of Costa Rica have countless activities and amusements from which to choose, including scuba diving, fishing, golfing, kayaking, hiking, surfing, swimming, and, of course, sightseeing. Cities contain excellent restaurants, and offer a variety of entertainment from small bars to exciting discotheques. Most hotels contain casinos. Along with all this there is astonishingly beautiful nature to see, from Amazon and Swiss alpine forests to dry savannas and towering volcanoes. It has been estimated that about 5% of the world's biodiversity — plants and animals — are found in Costa Rica.

History and Government

Before the Spanish arrived in 1502, Costa Rica was inhabited by the Guaymi Indians. After their arrival, the Spanish organized Costa Rica as a Spanish colony and the land remained that way until independence in 1821. For a brief period Costa Rica was a member of the Central American Federation but the country seceded in 1838. Except for a civil war, 1948-1949, the country has been remarkably stable. Clearly, its stability and enduring democracy have enabled Costa Rica to achieve a relatively high standard of living.

Costa Rica is a democratic republic. Its constitution, adopted in 1949, is based on Spanish civil law. The chief of state and head of government is the president, who is elected for a four-year term by universal suffrage (18 years of age). A unicameral assembly is the legislative branch of the government, and the judicial system is headed by a supreme court.

The Economy of Costa Rica

Costa Rica's economy can best be described as progressive. Tourism, the export of coffee, bananas, and other agricultural products, furniture, food processing, textiles, fertilizers, and cement are vital parts of the economy.

If there is a tarnished spot on Costa Rica's image, it is the current economy. The nation's debt is among the world's highest (based on the size of the country's GDP), inflation was as high as 22.5% in 1995, and about 30% of the country's families live in poverty. Aware of these problems, the government has taken steps to promote a healthy economy. The administration has instituted policies to reduce inflation, decrease the fiscal deficit, increase domestic savings, and improve the efficiency of the public sector. It also aims to increase the role of the private sector.

The currency of Costa Rica is the Costa Rican colon, which is easily exchanged for other currencies. Major credit cards are readily accepted at various locations.

Overall, Costa Rica's infrastructure is sound. The country has 13 major airports, several seaports — Caldera, Golfito, Moin, Puerto Limon, Puerto Quepos, and Puntarenas — and an excellent telecommunications system. International callers enjoy connection to Central American Microwave System and satellite earth station. Although many of Costa Rica's roads are unpaved, its cities are connected by paved highways. The Pan American Highway runs through the country, north to south.

Residence Havens

Tax Facts of Interest

Costa Rica is not as advantageous in regard to tax benefits as some other retirement havens. However, it does offer some significant benefits. <u>The rates for payment of income taxes are lower than in most developed countries and there is no tax on foreign-source income</u>. This can be extremely beneficial to the retired individual who maintains assets outside of the country.

Should you be interested in finding out more information about Costa Rica, contact:

The Embassy of Costa Rica
2114 S Street NW
Washington, DC 20008
Tel: 202-234-2945
Fax: 202-265-4795

U.S. Embassy (in San Jose, Costa Rica)
APO AA 34020
Tel: 506-220-3939
Fax: 506-220-2305

Costa Rican Investment and Trade Development Board
CINDE Building
La Uruca, San Jose
Costa Rica
Tel: 506-220-0036; 506-220-0366; 506-220-4755
Fax: 506-220-4754; 506-220-4750; 506-220-4752

Costa Rican Investment and Trade Development Board
CINDE/USA
90 West Street, Suite 614
New York, NY 10006
Tel: 212-964-1774
Fax: 212-964-1969

Cyprus

Cyprus, formally known as the Republic of Cyprus, is an island of the Middle East, located in the Mediterranean Sea, south of Turkey. Its nearest neighbors are Turkey to the north, and Syria and Lebanon to the east.

A rather small island, slightly less in area than the state of Connecticut, Cyprus's most distinguishing topographical features are the two mountain ranges that run east to west, separated by a wide fertile plain. The island's highest point is Olympus at close to 6,440 feet (1,952 meters). The island has an area of 3,572 square miles (about 9,250 square kilometers).

Cyprus has a temperate, Mediterranean climate. Its summers are hot and dry, and its winters are cool and wet. The average annual temperature of the island is 69 degrees F (about 21 degrees C). Annual rainfall averages about 20 inches (50 centimeters). Overall, the extremes between the seasons are rather unremarkable.

About 745,000 people live on Cyprus, the population being comprised mostly of Greeks and Turks. Greeks make up 78% of the population, while Turks account for 18%. Other minority groups account for the remaining 4%. It is important to realize that most Greeks (about 99%) live in the Greek area of the country, while close to 99% of the Turks live in Turkish area. The major religions of Cyprus include Greek Orthodox, to which about 78% of the population belongs, Muslim 18%, and Maronite, Armenian Apostolic, Roman Catholics, Jews, and others making up the rest. Greek, Turkish, and English are the major languages. The country's literacy rate is 94%.

Cyprus has adequate health care, with higher quality being found in cities. Life expectancy rates are good. Males are expected to live about 74 years while females can expect to live 79.

Residence Havens

Once considered a "developing" country, Cyprus shed that designation in mid-1991 when the World Bank took the island off its developing country list. Today Cyprus is a prosperous island nation in which residents enjoy a life style of good quality.

History and Government

Cyprus's history begins in prehistory. Archeological excavations show that advanced civilizations thrived on the island as far back as the Neolithic and Bronze ages. Cyprus's recorded history began about 1450 B.C. when Egypt occupied at least a part of the island. During the following centuries, various seafaring people established settlements along the island's coasts, mostly to facilitate trade. The first Greek colony appeared about 1,400 B.C., and the first Phoenician settlement was established about 800 B.C. Subsequently, Cyprus fell under the control of the dominant power of the Mediterranean at various times, including the Greeks, Persians, Egyptians, and Romans. In 1191, the island was seized by Richard I of England, who gave it to Jerusalem. In time, control of Cyprus passed to Venice and then Turkey, which eventually petitioned the British to administer the island in hopes of checking Russia's desire to expand southward. The British maintained administrative control until 1946 when they proposed constitutional reforms that would lead to self-government for the island. Independence was officially achieved in August, 1960.

Through much of its recent history, Greeks and Turks have had their differences. Unfortunately, these differences have sometimes erupted in to violence, one of the most notable events being a Turkish invasion of the island in July, 1974.

Cyprus is a republic, based on a constitution written in August of 1960. The chief of state and head of the government is the president, who is elected for a five-year term by universal suffrage. Citizens 18 years and older enjoy the right to vote. The legislative branch of the government is composed of a House of Representatives in the Greek area and an Assembly of the Republic in the Turkish area. The island's legal system is based on common law.

The Economy of Cyprus

Cyprus's economy is small and relatively prosperous, however, because of its size and components it is subject to instability. Although industry and the service sectors are important parts of the island's economy, the economy is dependent on agriculture and governmental services which together employ close to 50% of the nation's workforce. Tourism is growing, but does not approach a level where it has become an economic strength. In an attempt to support the country's economy the government provides significant aid to the various economic sectors. While the short-term gain of this strategy is obvious, the long-term effects are that inefficient enterprises are supported, relieving managers of implementing the types of changes that would in time lead to an overall healthier economy.

The official currency of Cyprus is the Cyprus pound. The banking system is similar to the English banking system in organization and services.

An important factor to any country's economic prospects is its infrastructure. Cyprus's infrastructure is quite sound. Its telephone system is rated excellent in both Greek and Turkish areas. Domestic service utilizes open wire, fiber-optic cable, and microwave radio relay. Cyprus is linked internationally via fiber-optic submarine cable and satellite. Indeed, the country's telecommunications system is considered to be one of the best in the world. The island has several seaports and two international airports. About half of its roads are paved.

Residence Havens

Tax Facts of Interest

Although Cyprus does not offer many tax incentives for individuals, the country offers various tax incentives for offshore companies. For some individuals, this option may prove extremely beneficial.

Offshore companies in Cyprus may be engaged in any of the following:

1 Providing management services.
2 Conducting business in transit operations and general trading.
3 Acting as a liaison for operations conducted in various territories.

Offshore companies may be eligible for various tax incentives, including:

- Limited companies enjoy a tax rate of 10% of normal rates, resulting in a tax rate which may be as low as 4.25%.
- Branches whose management and control is abroad pay no tax; when management and control are based in Cyprus the tax rate is 4.25%.
- Partnerships pay no tax.
- Dividends from offshore companies are not subject to additional taxes, either on the company or the recipient.
- No estate duties are required on the passing on of shares in a Cyprus offshore company held by individuals not domiciled in Cyprus because of death.
- No tax in payable by an offshore company on gains from the sale of real estate located outside Cyprus.

There are other benefits as well, not the least of which includes taking advantage of Cyprus's double tax treaties with various nations. Should you be interested in information regarding the establishment of an offshore company in Cyprus, contact the Central Bank of Cyprus, P.O. Box 5529 Nicosia-Cyprus. Tel: 02-445281. Fax: 02-472012.

Individuals who are considering retirement may take advantage of such tax incentives. After making the necessary investments, they might simply turn over the operation of a business to others while still benefiting from the incentives.

Should you be interested in finding out more about Cyprus, contact:

The Embassy of Cyprus
2211 R Street, NW
Washington, DC 20008
Tel: 202-462-5772

The Cyprus Tourism Organization
13 East 40th Street
New York, NY 10016
Tel: 212-683-5280
Fax: 212-683-5282

Cyprus Tourist Office
213 Regent Street
London W1, R8-DA
England
Tel: 071-734-9822
Fax: 071-287-6534

Cyprus Tourism Organization
D-600, 6, Frankfurt am Main 1
Kaiserstrasse 13
Germany
Tel: 069-284708
Fax: 069-293337

Residence Havens

*Cyprus Tourism Organization
36 Voukourestious Street
Athens
Greece
Tel: 3610178
Fax: 3644798*

*Cyprus Tourism Organization
83 Wetstraat
1040 Brussels
Belgium
Tel: 02-230-5984
Fax: 02-230-8578*

*Cyprus Tourism Organization
Palais France Building, 729
1-61 Jingumae
Shibuya-Ku
Tokyo
Japan
Tel: 03-34979329
Fax: 03-34050105*

Dubai

Dubai is one of the seven autonomous states of the United Arab Emirates, which stretch along the southern coast of the Persian Gulf. Dubai, a relatively small state, is bordered by Qatar on the north, Saudi Arabia on the west and south, and Oman on the east. Dubai's land is barren and flat, dominated by empty desert in the south.

Lying in a subtropical, arid zone, Dubai's climate is highlighted by hot, humid summers and mild, pleasant winters. The state receives only a few inches of rain each year.

Of the approximately 2,800,000 people that make up the United Arab Emirates, Dubai is home to about 530,000. Although the land is Arabic in history and culture, a significant percentage of Dubai's population is comprised of foreigners who have come to the state to find employment in Dubai's rapidly expanding economy. Most of these workers, who come from around the world — but most notably India, Iran, Europe and other Arab countries — reside in the cities.

Unquestionably, Dubai enjoys a prime location on the crossroads between East and West. Not only does the state possess enviable petroleum reserves, it is developing itself as a manufacturing site which will enable companies to tap the enormous and expanding consumer market of 1.4 billion people who live in the countries that surround the Gulf and Red Sea.

Arabic, of course, is the official language of Dubai. However, English is spoken widely and both Arabic and English are commonly used in business.

The quality of health care in Dubai is among the best in the Gulf. Hospitals and clinics boast modern equipment and well trained staff, and they provide effective treatment of virtually any disorder. Life expectancy is good, being 70 years for men and 74 years for women.

While the literacy rate of the general population is about 70%, the government has taken steps to improve the quality of the state's educational system. The literacy rate and education of foreigners in the country tends to be very high.

Many people are unfamiliar with Dubai and the fine lifestyle it can offer. Numerous activities are available, including: swimming, sailing, water-skiing, scuba diving, golf, soccer, cricket, tennis, and horse and camel racing. Superior hotels, restaurants, and nightclubs are located in the emirate. Most people are also not aware that Dubai is the site of the Jebel Ali Free Zone, which is the largest commercial and industrial free zone in the Middle East. The Jebel Ali Free Zone offers some of the best tax incentives in the world. Astute retirees who wish to invest some of their assets can be eligible for many of these benefits.

History and Government

Since the dawning of recorded history, Dubai has been a trading center that has seen goods pass through on their way to destinations in the Far East, India, and Africa. Indeed, until 1966 and the discovery of oil, Dubai's economy depended entirely on trade. Oil is now black gold to the state. Within just a few years of the discovery of oil, the profits from the fuel enabled Dubai's leaders to implement countless construction projects in which the state's infrastructure was expanded and modernized.

Dubai is one of the seven states that make up the United Arab Emirates, a federation that was formed in 1971 when Great Britain, which had controlled the region, withdrew from the area. Dubai is the second largest of the emirates.

The federation has been good for the region, as it has brought stability and economic expansion to this part of the Arab world.

The Economy of Dubai

Supported by oil reserves, Dubai has a strong economy. The state's leaders, however, aware that oil reserves are projected to last only another 30 years, have wisely embarked upon a major diversification program which they hope will result in Dubai developing industries and commercial enterprises that will eventually take the place of oil as the predominate commodity of the state's economy. Already this policy has brought positive results as Dubai is recognized as a prominent industrial and commercial site of the region.

Nowhere is this policy more apparent than in Dubai's infrastructure, which is one of the most modern of the Gulf region and which ranks as one of the best in the world. Telecommunications, ports, and roads are among the best of the entire region. Dubai International Airport handles over 55 airlines, averaging close to 150 flights per day. The Jebel Ali Seaport, the largest man-made harbor in the world, is one of the most advanced and efficient in the world. It is linked directly to the Jebel Ali Free Zone.

Dubai's banking system is designed to provide the various services both businesses and consumers require. Dubai's currency is the Dirham, which is easily exchanged for other currencies. The state welcomes investors and entrepreneurs.

Tax Facts of Interest

Any tax advantages Dubai offers are connected to the Jebel Ali Free Zone. The free zone was created in 1985 in an effort to diversify and strengthen Dubai's economic base. This free zone offers facilities to satisfy the needs of virtually every business and industrial enterprise. The free zone is also noted for the considerable incentives it offers, most importantly that <u>companies operating in the zone are not required to pay personal or corporate taxes for a period of 15 years. In addition, this 15-year period is renewable for another 15 years.</u>

There are other incentives as well. Companies and their managers are limited by few restrictions in a liberal business climate. There are no requirements that force companies to enter in to partnerships with local enterprises, no import or export duties are payable within the zone, there is 100% repatriation of both profit and capital within the zone, and there are no restrictions on currency. The advantages offered by the Jebel Ali Free Zone to those considering retirement, and who have assets they would like to invest in a state where their tax liabilities are limited, are quite obvious.

Should you like to find out more information about Dubai, contact:

The Dubai Commerce and Tourism Promotion Board
P.O. Box 594
Dubai
United Arab Emirates
Tel: 971-4-511600
Fax: 971-4-511711

Dubai Commerce and Tourism Promotion Board
8 Penn Center, 19th Floor
Philadelphia, PA 19103
USA
Tel: 215-751-9750
Fax: 215-751-9551

Dubai Commerce and Tourism Promotion Board
Neue Mainzer Strasse
57, D 60311 Frankfurt/Main
Germany
Tel: 4969-253422
Fax: 4969-253151

Dubai Commerce and Tourism Promotion Board
Suite 1102
38 Gloucester Road
Hong Kong
Tel: 00852-28029002
Fax: 00852-28272511

Ecuador

    Ecuador, the smallest of the Andean countries, is located in northwestern South America. The Pacific Ocean meets Ecuador on the west, Colombia lies to the north, and Peru borders the country on the east and south. Slightly smaller than the state of Nevada, Ecuador's area is about 109,480 square miles (283,560 square kilometers). The Galapagos Islands in the Pacific, about 600 miles (965 kilometers) to the west belong to Ecuador.

    The country has varying topography and may be divided into four distinct regions: the coastal plain, the Sierra (or central highlands), the Oriente (eastern jungle), and the Galapagos Islands. On either side of the central plateau are massive mountains, the highest being Cotopaxi at 19,347 feet (5,897 meters), which also is the highest active volcano in the world.

    Despite lying on the equator, which the name Ecuador implies, the varying altitudes of Ecuador's land result in a wide range of climates. Along the coast, the typical weather is hot and humid. Average annual temperatures here are about 78 degrees F (26 degrees C). In the mountains average temperatures range between 45 and 70 degrees F (7 and 21 degrees C). The Oriente is extremely humid and hot; here temperatures throughout the year average about 100 degrees F (38 degrees C). The Oriente is also the wettest environment in Ecuador, often receiving up to 80 inches (200 centimeters) of rainfall per year. Most other areas of the country have wet and dry seasons.

    Ecuador has about 11,500,000 people. Its ethnic divisions mirror those of most Latin American countries in general groups if not actual percentages, being comprised of Mestizos, 55%, Indians, 25%, Spanish, 10%, and blacks, 10%. The predominate religion is Roman Catholicism with 95% of the people belonging to this faith. While Spanish is the official language, and the primary language of most of the population, Quechua and other Indian languages are also spoken. The literacy rate of the country is about 90%. It is noteworthy, however, that only about 33% of the people in rural areas complete sixth grade while in urban areas this number is 76%.

Like many developing countries around the world, Ecuador's major cities offer the best living standards of the country. This includes education and health care. In the cities and important towns health care is considered adequate to very good; in outlying areas the quality of health care diminishes. The life expectancy rate for men is 67 years and for women it is 73.

Ecuador is a country that offers some of the most beautiful sites in South America. Quito, the capital, is one of them. Located near the equator, but about 9,100 feet (2,850 meters) in elevation, the city enjoys a year-round, springlike climate. Situated in a valley between mountains, Quito's people are able to see several snowcapped volcanoes from various locations throughout the city. The city, itself, is a mix of old and new with a center that is filled with colonial buildings. Modern architecture is limited to only certain areas.

Visitors to Ecuador may travel through picturesque valleys on their way along the Pan American Highway to see towering volcanoes, trek through Amazon rainforest, or browse historic sites and museums. Natural history lovers will enjoy visiting the Galapagos Islands, which are known the world over for their marine and bird wildlife. Mountain climbing, trekking, scuba diving, and beach-going are some other recreational activities one may pursue in Ecuador.

History and Government

Although much of Ecuador's earliest history is lost within the mists of time, there is archeological evidence indicating that the first Native Americans settled in the region around 12,000 B.C. It is also believed that Polynesians reached coastal areas about this time, or not long after. Various tribes inhabited the area in relative peace for centuries before the arrival of the Incas around 1450. The Incas were conquerors, and despite strong opposition they subjugated the tribes that lived in Ecuador, holding the region until the Spanish conquistador Pizarro destroyed their empire soon after reaching the country in 1532.

The Spanish ruled Ecuador as a colony for the next 300 years. Simon Bolivar, the freedom fighter, liberated the land in 1822, and the country gained full independence in 1830.

Throughout the remainder of the 19th century, and much of the 20th, Ecuador has experienced violence and political instability. Indeed, this century has seen more military intervention and rule than civilian rule. Although Ecuador's border with Peru remains in dispute (in 1941 Peru invaded Ecuador over the country's Amazon territory), the last several years have been peaceful and many now believe Ecuador to be one of the safest and most stable in South America.

Despite its past in which military dictatorships often seized power, today Ecuador is a republic. The chief of state and head of the government is the president, who is elected for a four-year term. Suffrage is universal for people 18 years of age, compulsory for literate individuals between the ages of 18 and 65, and optional for other voters. The National Congress is the country's legislative branch; the court system is based on civil law, embodied in the Constitution of 1979.

The Economy of Ecuador

Ecuador's economy is built around substantial oil reserves and its rich agricultural regions. The country's chief crops include bananas, which are its largest export, coffee, rice, and sugar. While Ecuador possesses mineral wealth

— most notably copper, iron, lead, silver, and sulfur — oil is by far the most important resource.

In recent years, Ecuador's economy has been somewhat uneven because of fluctuations in the prices for the country's principal exports of oil and bananas. Inflation has also been a worry, with the rate being as high as 55% in 1992. Government action to decrease the inflation rate — which has been somewhat successful, slowing inflation to 25% by 1995 — unfortunately, has also dampened the economy. Recent estimates of the inflation rate are about 23%. The current administration hopes to spur economic growth by encouraging foreign investment.

The country's economy is further hampered by Ecuador's infrastructure. Throughout much of the country, the telephone system is generally considered to be unreliable and inadequate, especially for the telecommunications needs of a modern, global economy. Electric power also must be expanded and modernized. The economy's growth rate of just 2.3% in 1995 was in part a result of shortages of electricity. Of the nation's total of 26,220 miles of highways (43,700 kilometers), only about 3,150 miles (5,245 kilometers) are paved. Some parts of the country are virtually inaccessible by motor vehicle. While Ecuador has several ports and airports, most need to be modernized.

The sucre is the currency of Ecuador. It may be readily exchanged for U.S. dollars, which go a long way in the country. Americans visiting Ecuador will be surprised at the country's low costs of living compared to the costs in the U.S. A restaurant meal, for example, may cost little more than two dollars and a good hotel room costs about four dollars.

Tax Facts of Interest

Although no special tax concessions are granted to foreign nationals, Ecuador's tax laws are favorable to individuals who maintain sources of income

Ecuador

outside of the country. Ecuador taxes its citizens and foreign nationals on Ecuadorian-source income. This income is defined as income derived from activities conducted in Ecuador.

<u>Individuals are not taxed on foreign-source income. Thus, any income earned abroad from any non-Ecuadorian related activity is not considered taxable. This includes dividends, pensions, interest income, and other similar sources.</u> This is extremely noteworthy to the retired person who maintains sources of income outside the country.

<u>In addition, there are no provincial, county, or municipal taxes levied in Ecuador. Nor are there any special taxes associated with wealth. Taxes on inheritance, gifts, and donations apply only on assets located in Ecuador.</u>

When these tax provisions are added to the generally low costs of living in Ecuador, it quickly becomes clear that Ecuador is potentially an excellent retirement haven.

Ecuador welcomes visitors from around the world. Travelers from the U.S. don't require a visa unless they expect to remain in Ecuador for more than 90 days. Visitors from other countries should contact the Embassy of Ecuador or the nearest Ecuadorian Consulate for travel information.

Should you be interested in more information about Ecuador, contact the following:

Embassy of Ecuador
2535 15th St., NW
Washington, DC 20009
Tel: 202-234-7200
Fax: 202-667-3482

Consulate of Ecuador
800 Second Ave., Suite 601
New York, NY 10017
Tel: 212-808-0170 or 212-808-0171
Fax: 212-808-0188

Consulate of Ecuador
B.I.V. Tower
1101 Brickell Ave., Suite M-102
Miami, FL 33131
Tel: 305-539-8214/15
Fax: 305-539-8313

Consulate of Ecuador
500 North Michigan Ave., Suite 1510
Chicago, IL 60611
Tel: 312-329-0266
Fax: 312-329-0359

Consulate of Ecuador
548 South Spring St., Suite 602
Los Angeles, CA 90013
Tel: 213-628-3014 or 213-628-3016
Fax: 213-689-8418

Consulate of Ecuador
Calle Recinto Sur 301
Oficina 401-A
San Juan, PR 00901
Casilla Postal 4542
San Juan, PR 00905
Tel: 809-724-2356
Fax: 809-724-2356

Ecuador

Consulate of Ecuador
1010 St. Catherine Quest, Suite 440
P.O. Box H3B3R3
Montreal, Quebec H3B3R3
Canada
Tel: 514-874-4071
Fax: 514-931-0252

Consulate of Ecuador
151 Bloor St., West, Suite 470
Toronto, Ontario M5S1S4
Canada
Tel: 416-968-2077
Fax: 416-968-3348

Greece

The Republic of Greece is located in southeastern Europe, at the southernmost part of the Balkan Peninsula. Along with its territory on the peninsula, the republic includes numerous small islands. The Aegean Sea, Ionian Sea, and Mediterranean Sea all wash upon Greece's shores. On the northwest, the country is bordered by Albania, on the north by Yugoslavia and Bulgaria, and on the northeast by Turkey. Slightly smaller than Alabama, Greece is 50,944 square miles (131,944 square kilometers). About one-fifth of its land area is composed of islands in the Aegean and Ionian seas.

Greece is known for its natural beauty. Rugged, mountainous land is surrounded by the sea that presses in on it with countless bays and inlets. For a relatively small country, Greece possesses wondrous topography. A central mountain region looms through the country north to south and contains Mount Olympus, which was once thought to be the home of the gods of the ancient Greeks. At 9,770 feet (2,917 meters) high, Olympus reigns over the rest of the country, much of which consists of plains and valleys flanked by mountains. The islands of Greece tend to be mountainous and sparsely inhabited.

Greece's climate is temperate with mild, wet winters and hot, dry summers. The mean annual temperature in Athens is about 63 degrees F (17 degrees C). In January, the normal low is about 31 degrees F (-0.6 degrees C), while in July the normal high is about 99 degrees F (37.2 degrees C). Summers, especially in the lowlands, are usually hot and dry with abundant blue skies. Average annual temperatures, of course, vary with elevation, although only areas in the highest mountains may be thought of as being cool. Rainfall varies throughout the country depending upon location. Generally, parts of the west coast receive the most rainfall.

Residence Havens

About 10,540,000 people live in Greece. The population is close to 98% Greek with the remainder being comprised of Turks, Macedonian Slavs, Albanians, Armenians, and Bulgarians. Most of the people belong to the Greek Orthodox church (98%), with Muslim's (1.3%) being the second largest religious group. Greek, of course, is the country's official language, however English and French are also rather common. The country's literacy rate is 98%.

The standard of living in Greece compares favorably with other countries of southeastern Europe. Although the quality of health care is good in the major cities, adequate care declines as one ventures into the more isolated spots of the country. Nevertheless, overall life expectancy is good: 75 years for men and 81 years for women.

Greece is a country of marvelous beauty and history. The land was home to one of the first great civilizations of Europe and many of our governmental institutions, philosophies, even the original roots of many common words in English can be traced to the ancient Greeks. Visiting some of the ruins from those days can be an experience that will be remembered throughout one's life.

History and Government

Greece's history begins in Neolithic times. The many natural harbors along the coasts of the country together with the many islands throughout the Aegean Sea made ancient Greece a center of early Mediterranean maritime civilization. Goods, along with ideas, flowed to and from Greece. As early as 2,000 B.C. maritime civilization throughout the Aegean had progressed to a rather high level of sophistication.

While the sea provided Greece contact with other people, the formidable mountains and valleys of the country divided the land into parts and helped to foster the development of independent city states. Places like Athens, Sparta, Corinth, and Ithaca are well known both in history and Greek mythology.

Originally ruled by kings, the governments of the city-states eventually came to be managed by oligarchies, and from there democracies. It is thought that Athens was the first city-state to embrace democratic rule.

Ancient Greece has a long and fascinating history. From about 1,200 B.C. — the approximate date of the Trojan War described by Homer in his *Iliad* — to about 200 B.C. when the Romans began to take an interest in Greek affairs that eventually led to the assimilation of Greece into the Roman Empire, Greece played a dominant role in the Mediterranean region.

After the Romans, Greece had various masters, including French, Spanish, Italian, and Ottoman rulers. Nationalism began to grow into a powerful force under the Ottomans, but it was not until 1829 that Greek independence was attained.

Modern Greece is a parliamentary republic with its capital at Athens. The chief of state is the president who is elected by popular vote of citizens 18 years of age and older. The head of the government is the prime minister, who is appointed by the president. A cabinet is also appointed by the president, on the recommendation of the prime minister. The legislative branch of the government is a unicameral Chamber of Deputies. Based on codified Roman law, the judiciary is divided into civil, criminal, and administrative courts. Greece's constitution was accepted on June 11, 1975.

The Economy of Greece

While capitalism is strong in Greece's economy, the public sector constitutes a major part of the country's GDP, about 70% as of 1989. Greece's overall economy has been weak in recent years, averaging less than 2% in terms of real GDP growth. A member of the EU, Greece is striving to meet the EU criteria for participating in economic and monetary programs. Currently, the country relies on the EU for vital aid.

Residence Havens

Despite slow economic growth, there is cause for optimism. Tourism has grown as an important part of the country's economy and is a major source of foreign exchange, agriculture is generally self-sufficient, and industrial output has been rising. Along with tourism and agriculture, Greece's major industries include tobacco processing, textiles, chemicals, metal products, mining, and petroleum.

Greece's infrastructure can be described as adequate. The country possesses modern telephone networks that reach virtually all regions, and there is an impressive open wire network. International communications are carried over submarine cables as well as satellites. An extensive highway system, airports and seaports provide reliable transportation. Indeed, 77 airports and 12 seaports are located around Greece. The seaports, in particular, are well-developed.

Greece also has a well-developed system of banking, which includes a central bank, several commercial banks, investment banks, credit institutions, and branch offices of foreign banks. The drachma is the country's currency.

Tax Facts of Interest

A cursory glance at Greece's tax laws would dismiss the country as being a retirement haven. For most people, the tax laws in Greece are burdensome. There are a variety of taxes, including income tax, real estate transfer tax, real property tax, inheritance tax, and seemingly countless other minor taxes. However, under Law 89 of the Greek tax code, under the title "Establishment in Greece of Foreign Commercial and Industrial Companies," significant tax exemptions may be obtained.

<u>Most importantly, any foreign commercial or industrial company that establishes a regional office in Greece receives a 100% exemption from income tax, as well as being eligible for other tax benefits.</u> To be sure, specific steps must be followed to secure the exemptions.

Greece

First, the establishment of a Greek regional office is subject to the approval of the Minister of Coordination. This approval comes only after power of attorney is granted to a permanent Greek resident who will then act as the foreign company's legal representative. Furthermore, it is required by law that a Greek consular officer in the home country of the foreign company authenticate the power of attorney. In addition, the foreign parent company will usually be required to file documentation including a copy of its annual balance sheet and profit and loss statement, as well as its articles of incorporation. All this, of course, is to ensure that only legitimate companies take advantage of the tax exemptions.

Thousands of companies, especially those that operate shipping fleets, have established Greek regional offices to take advantage of the tax benefits, which apply to non-Greek source income from around the world.

The company owner who wishes to retire — or perhaps semi-retire — can easily see the excellent advantages here. After establishing a Greek regional office, he or she may hand day-to-day control of the company to someone else while continuing to benefit from its operations.

Following is a list of the major tax benefits a foreign regional office that functions under Law 89, and which derives no income from Greece, is eligible for:

- Exemption from all Greek taxes.

- Exemption from income tax on the earnings of foreign personnel who work for the regional office.

- Exemption from all customs duties, import taxes, stamp duties, and luxury taxes on items imported to equip the regional office.

- Exemption from duties on the importation of items necessary to furnish the home of the regional office's foreign personnel.

Residence Havens

- Exemption from any export-import duties that might otherwise be levied on samples of advertising material by the regional office.

- Exemption from tax on interest received from deposits in Greek banks.

- Exemption from interest received from government bonds.

- Exemption for certain operations from a tax on the profits from the sale of securities.

- Exemption from any tax on the interest from loans granted by foreign banks or firms to certain Greek entities.

- Exemption from duties on the conversion of bond or preference shares of corporations, and also on the replacement of shares of bond certificates.

Should you be interested in more information about Greece, contact:

The Embassy of Greece
2221 Massachusetts Ave., NW
Washington, DC 20008
Tel: 202-939-5800
Fax: 202-939-5824

The Greek National Tourist Organization
645 Fifth Ave.
Olympic Tower
New York, NY 10022
Tel: 212-421-5757

The Greek National Tourist Organization
Amerikis St.
Athens, Greece
Tel: 01-322-3111/9

The Embassy of the United States in Greece
Mailing address: PSC 108, APO AE 09842
Tel: 30-1-721-2951,8401
Fax: 30-1-645-6282

Note: The Greek National Tourist Organization maintains offices in many cities around the world. Check local phone directories for current numbers.

Guatemala

Guatemala is located in the northern part of Central America. It is bordered by Mexico to the north and northwest, Belize to the east, and Honduras and El Salvador on the south. Guatemala has access to the Pacific Ocean from its western coast and the Atlantic through the Gulf of Honduras. The central part of the country is highland and mountain areas, which give way to the narrow Pacific coast and the lowlands to the east. Guatemala is 42,042 square miles (108,890 square kilometers), about the size of Tennessee. Several volcanoes are found throughout the southern part of Guatemala, with Volcan Tajumulco at 13,845 feet (4,220 meters) being the country's highest point. Volcanic eruptions and earthquakes are not unusual.

The climate of Guatemala is tropical. Lowland areas are hot and humid, while the highlands and mountain regions are cooler. Taking advantage of these cooler temperatures, much of the population lives between 3,000 and 8,000 feet (915 and 2,440 meters) above sea level. At these elevations the days are generally warm and the nights cool, with the average annual temperatures hovering around 68 degrees F (20 degrees C). The average temperatures in the lowlands are much more tropical, highlighted with heat and high humidity. Guatemala has a rainy season from May to October and a dry season from November to April. Overall, the country receives an ample amount of rain, averaging about 50 inches (130 centimeters) in the south to over 100 inches (254 centimeters) in some parts of the north.

Guatemala's population is slightly over 11,200,000. Mestizos account for 56% of the country's people while Native Americans comprise the remaining 44%. In the local Spanish, Mestizos are called Ladino. There are few minority groups in the country.

Although Spanish is the official language, it is spoken by only about 60% of the population. A variety of Indian languages are spoken by the rest of the country's people. There are 23 major Indian dialects, including Quiche, Cakchiquel, and Kekchi. Many of these languages are derived from the original Mayan inhabitants of the region.

Roman Catholicism is the dominant religion, however, there are Protestant groups. Some people adhere to traditional Mayan beliefs.

Guatemala is a relatively poor country that trails developed countries in the quality of health care, education, and life style it can offer to most of its people. Life expectancy for men is 63 years and for women it is 70 years. Of the general population, about 60% have access to health care. The literacy rate is only 56%. The best quality of life, of course, can be found in Guatemala City, which is the country's capital. Far from major cities and towns, conditions in isolated regions can be quite primitive.

Over the years, a goal of many Guatemalan governments has been to close the gap between rich and poor. Unfortunately, this gap remains, making uneven distribution of wealth a serious problem for the country. Much of the problem has its beginnings during Spanish colonization when wealthy Spaniards controlled vast tracts of land. Modern Guatemalan society is still trying to rectify the results of those days.

Why then might someone considering retirement even think of Guatemala? There are several reasons. Despite the country's struggle to provide its people with improved living standards, Guatemala has much to offer. The pre-Columbian Mayan world, the colonial days of Spanish control, and an evolving society that is striving forward have all come together to make Guatemala a diverse and exciting nation.

Guatemala City is unquestionably modern and cosmopolitan. The city is a mix of the old and new, where one can experience the culture of the Mayans as it has been handed down through the centuries and yet enjoy the comforts of a modern world. In addition to this, the country does have some tax exemptions which some people considering retirement might find advantageous.

History and Government

A thousand years before the arrival of the Spanish, Mayan civilization flourished throughout the land that has become Guatemala. After the Spanish conquest, Guatemala remained a Spanish colony from 1524-1821. It briefly became a part of Mexico, and then became a member of the United States of Central America, finally establishing itself as a republic in 1839. Guatemala has been a sovereign state since then.

Throughout its history, Guatemala has suffered a succession of civilian governments, dictatorships, and military takeovers. It has been difficult for a tradition of democracy to be established.

Modern Guatemala is a republic, based on a constitution that took effect on January 14, 1986. The chief of state and head of the government is the president, who is elected for a four-year term by universal suffrage. To assist in governing, the president names a Council of Ministers. Guatemala's legislative branch of government is a unicameral Congress of the Republic, and the country's judiciary is based on a system of civil law.

The Economy of Guatemala

Guatemala's economy centers around farming. Family and corporate agriculture accounts for 25% of the country's GDP, employs 3 out of 5 Guatemalans, and supplies about 65% of the country's exports. Sugarcane, coffee, bananas, corn, and beans are some of Guatemala's most important agricultural products. Along with the crops noted, beef is also an important export.

Residence Havens

Although manufacturing accounts for about 20% of the GDP, most production facilities are small. Manufacturing employs only 14% of the labor force.

Because of the general weakness of the economy, Guatemala's unemployment rate remains high at about 13%. Moreover, it is estimated that 30% to 40% of those with jobs are underemployed.

Outside of the capital city, much of Guatemala's infrastructure needs improvement. While the telephone system is generally modern in Guatemala City, there are only an estimated 210,000 phones in the country even though there are over 11,000,000 Guatemalans. Roadways in and near the capital are generally good, but as one drives farther from the city, road conditions may deteriorate. The country possesses five ports and numerous airports. Of the airports, however, none can be considered to possess state-of-the-art facilities.

Guatemala City enjoys a modern system of banking. While other parts of the country have access to modern banking, too, the activity of financial institutions is greatest around population centers. The currency of Guatemala is the quetzal.

Tax Facts of Interest

Although Guatemala, as is the case in many Latin American countries, has numerous taxes, there are some potentially valuable exclusions. Income tax, which is calculated from gross income, excludes interest from bonds or titles of the government and its agencies, dividends, including stock dividends, and benefits which had already been taxed in another form in the same period. More importantly, Guatemala follows the Latin American tradition of only taxing income from sources within the country, so a person living in Guatemala with all of their income coming from abroad is totally exempt. For some individuals, these exclusions can lead to large tax savings.

Should you be interested in more information about Guatemala, contact:

The Embassy of Guatemala
2220 R St., NW
Washington, DC 20008
Tel: 202-745-4952-4
Fax: 202-745-1908

Guatemala Tourist Commission
Seventh Ave.
1-7 Centro Civico
Guatemala City
Guatemala
Tel: 31-13-33/47

The Embassy of Guatemala
Carretera 175, K. 11.7
Carraizo Bajo
Trujillo, Puerto Rico
Tel: 809-760-1001
Fax: 809-749-9877

The Embassy of Guatemala
294 Alberto St., Suite 500
Ottawa, Ontario KIP 636
Canada
Tel: 613-224-4322
Fax: 613-237-0492

The Embassy of Guatemala
Zeitenstrasse 16, D-5300
Bonn 2
Federal Republic of Germany
Tel: 228-358609, 351848, 351579
Fax: 228-354940

The Embassy of Guatemala
Calle Rafael Salgado 3, 40. izquierda.
Madrid 16
Spain
Tel: 1-4577827, 2504035, 2500218
Fax: 1-4587894

The Embassy of Guatemala
13 Fawcett St.
London SW 10
Great Britain
Tel: 1-3513042
Fax: 1-376-5708

The Embassy of Guatemala
Kowa Nr. 38 Bldg. Rm. 905, 12-24
Nichi-Azabu
4-Chome, Minato-Ku
Tokyo 106
Japan
Tel: 3-4001830, 4001820
Fax: 3-34001820

Honduras

Honduras is located in Central America, between Guatemala to the north and Nicaragua to the south. It has access to both the Caribbean Sea and the Pacific Ocean. Honduras is 43,277 square miles (112,090 square kilometers), slightly larger than Tennessee, and is mountainous with thick forests and wide, fertile valleys. Forests cover over 40% of the country and yield valuable hardwoods and softwoods. Its mountains, which are volcanic in origin, rise over 9,000 feet (about 2,800 meters).

The climate of Honduras varies with elevation. In the lowlands along the coasts the climate is subtropical, while in the plateaus and mountains it is temperate. In the coastal regions the average annual temperature is 80 degrees F (26.7 degrees C); high humidity is the norm. The average temperatures in the mountains are about ten degrees cooler and the humidity is less oppressive. A dry season lasts from November to May. Like temperature, rainfall also varies according to elevation. The coastal lowlands may receive up to 100 inches (254 centimeters) of rain per year while mountain areas may receive about 40 inches (about 100 centimeters).

Honduras has a population of 5,600,000. About 90% of its people are Mestizo, with Indians, 7%, blacks, 2%, and whites, 1%, comprising the rest of the population. Based on these percentages, Honduras has one of the largest Mestizo populations of Latin America. The vast majority of Hondurans, about 97%, are Roman Catholics, with most of the rest belonging to Protestant denominations. Spanish is the official language of the country, however, several Indian dialects are widely spoken. English is also widely spoken, especially in the capital city of Tegucigalpa. The literacy rate is just over 70%, with the greatest illiteracy being in remote areas.

Residence Havens

Like most developing countries, Honduras struggles to provide quality health care to all of its people. While health care is considered to be adequate to good in major towns and cities, the quality of care declines as one moves into less populated areas. Life expectancy for men is 66 years and for women 70. It should be noted that, if necessary, specialized health care may be obtained in Miami, New Orleans, or Houston, which are only two hours travel time by air from Honduras. It is also noteworthy that many Honduran doctors and dentists receive training in the U.S. and Europe.

Although Honduras is one of the poorest countries in the Western Hemisphere, its poverty does not affect all parts of the country. There are plenty of excellent places to live, close to a wide variety of pleasurable activities. Spacious, well built homes, usually containing inner patios or atriums, abound in comfortable residential areas. Domestic help is easily obtained at modest rates.

Located near such residential areas are modern shopping malls and supermarkets that offer countless products much like those easily found in the U.S. Fine restaurants, theaters, and numerous activities including scuba diving, swimming, tennis, golf, fishing, and membership in prestigious country clubs make life interesting and pleasurable in Honduras. Cable TV and satellite TV are offered in principal cities.

History and Government

Long before the arrival of the Spanish, Honduras was the southern tip of the great Mayan civilization, which some historians believe dominated Central America for nearly a thousand years. By the time Columbus explored Trujillo in northeast Honduras in 1502 on his third voyage to the New World, the Mayan greatness had disappeared. After overcoming resistance by the Indian groups, including the descendants of the Mayans that inhabited the region, the Spanish settled Honduras, making it a part of their colonial empire. However, Spanish settlers brought few women with them, and they intermarried with Indian women, a practice that has resulted in Honduras's high percentage of Mestizos today.

Honduras remained a Spanish possession until 1821 when it gained its independence. The new country soon joined the Central American Federation, becoming independent again after the break-up of the federation in 1839.

Throughout its history, Honduras has struggled to install lasting democratic rule. The country has suffered through coups, dictatorships, and internal violence and repression. In 1989, with the election of a civilian president who was committed to modernizing the nation, Honduras seems to have embarked upon a program that diminishes the role of the military and expands the role of civilians in governing the country.

Honduras today is a stable democracy. The chief of state and head of the government is the president, who is elected to a four-year term by a simple majority of the people. Citizens 18 years of age and older enjoy the right to vote, which is universal and compulsory. The country's legislative branch is the National Congress, while the judiciary is based on Roman and Spanish civil law, with some influence of English common law.

The Economy of Honduras

Without question, Honduras is one of the poorest countries of the Western Hemisphere. However, the civilian government is committed to private enterprise and keenly aware of the need to initiate policies that will reduce the country's poverty. Agriculture dominates Honduras's economy, provides about 65% of the nation's jobs, and accounts for two-thirds of the country's exports. Coffee and bananas, both commodities prone to sharp price fluctuations, are the most important agricultural products. Manufacturing, which employs less than 10% of the labor force, and produces only 20% of the exports, suffers from low productivity and capital. Economic growth is undermined by a variety of problems, including: rapid population increase, high inflation (about 30%), high unemployment, an inadequate infrastructure (especially outside of the major cities), and an inefficient public sector.

Although these problems are serious, Honduras also has several factors that have the potential to help the economy grow. While telecommunications may be poor in outlying areas, they are relatively modern — capable of providing quality service — in the country's cities. Modern systems provide reliable phone, fax, and data transmissions.

Major transportation systems are good. Honduras has several seaports, of which Puerto Cortes is the only deep water port in all of Central America. It is also one of the region's largest and most modernized ports. In addition three other ports — Tela, La Ceiba, and Puerto Castillo — provide ocean access to the Atlantic, while Amapala provides access to the Pacific. Honduras also has four international airports that serve Tegucigalpa, the capital city. The country is self-sufficient in electricity and is able to export excess capacity. Being self-sufficient in energy is a major advantage to industry and the future of the country's economy.

In anticipation of the growing needs of business and consumers, Honduras is developing a modern financial system. About 20 private banks are currently operating in the country, including branches of Citibank and Lloyds Bank. Honduran banks offer the various services consumers and businesses in any advanced country expect and require. The Honduran currency is the lempira.

Based on the current conditions of Honduras's economy and the factors that will likely affect it in the coming years, it's clear that Honduras has much potential. Already today, despite the country's general poverty, there are modern, affluent areas that shine like jewels of what Honduras can become.

Tax Facts of Interest

Although Honduras has numerous taxes, it is noteworthy that <u>nonresident individuals domiciled in Honduras are subject to tax on income only from sources in Honduras. There is no tax on foreign-source income.</u>

Honduras also has free zones and Export Processing Zones (EPZ) that offer major tax incentives. For some individuals, these zones can provide excellent opportunities. The Honduran government has established Export Processing Zones at eight sites. Companies at these sites enjoy a variety of facilities, including:

- **Water, power, and communication services.**
- **Security.**
- **Waste collection and cleaning services.**
- **Legal services.**
- **In house customs services.**
- **Employment agency.**
- **Health clinic.**

Of most importance to many companies, however, are the tax advantages provided by EPZs. <u>A factory located in a Honduran EPZ pays no taxes of any kind. This includes income taxes, import and export taxes, and any other tax for as long as the factory remains in the EPZ.</u>

In addition, the owner of a factory in a Honduran EPZ enjoys these benefits as well:

- **Guarantee of private ownership and operation.**
- **Honduran registration of the plant is unnecessary.**

- **Imported materials and exported products are shipped rapidly into and out of the EPZ.**

- **Customs' clearances are simplified.**

- **No restrictions are in place regarding foreign exchange or the repatriation of capital or profits.**

An entrepreneur may wish to establish a factory in a Honduran EPZ, then turn over the daily operations to subordinates, in effect then enjoying a retirement that is supported by a company that profits through the tax advantages of the EPZ. This individual would also be able to enjoy the quality of Honduran life.

Should you be interested in finding out more information about Honduras, contact:

The Embassy of Honduras
3007 Tilden St., NW
Washington, DC 20008
Tel: 202-966-7702, 2604, 5008, 4596
Fax: 202-966, 9751

Consulate of Honduras
300 Sevilla Ave., Suite 201
Coral Gables, FL 33134
Tel: 305-447-8927

Hong Kong

Hong Kong, the former British dependency and marvelous economic success story, officially became reunited with China on July 1, 1997. Located in eastern Asia on the South China Sea, Hong Kong is composed of a portion of the mainland and many islands. Hong Kong can be divided into three main regions: Hong Kong Island and nearby islets, the Kowloon Peninsula and Stone cutters Island, and the New Territories, which are comprised mostly of land on the mainland and on Lan Tao Island. Much of Hong Kong is hilly, while the rest is lowland areas that meet the sea. Although it is quite small, 403 square miles (1045 square kilometers), making it about six times the size of Washington, DC, Hong Kong is a major economic power.

While it cannot be denied that the takeover by Communist China places a cloud over Hong Kong, no one at this time knows whether that cloud will bring a storm to the region or if it will part and permit the sun to continue to shine. At the time of this writing, Hong Kong remains an attractive retirement haven for a variety of reasons.

Hong Kong has a tropical monsoon climate. It is cool and humid in the winter and hot and rainy from spring through summer. While the best time of the year in Hong Kong is autumn when the weather tends to be warm and sunny, the overall climate of the region is quite nice. The average annual temperature is 72 degrees F (about 22 degrees C), ranging from an average high of 82 degrees F (28 degrees C) in July to an average low of 59 degrees F (15 degrees C) in February.

Slightly over 6,300,000 people live in Hong Kong. Although thousands of its residents emigrated before the reversion to Chinese control, the great majority of its people have stayed, which will help to ensure the prospects for the region's stability and continued economic success. About 95% of Hong Kong's residents are Chinese, with the remaining population being made up of various minorities. About 90% of the people belong to various local religions, with about 10% calling themselves Christian. The predominate languages are Chinese (Cantonese) and English. Hong Kong has a high rate of literacy at 92%.

In part because of British colonial rule and legacy, Hong Kong's system of health care is excellent. The area is one of the most modern in the world, its residence having access to the conveniences and standards of a highly developed country. Indeed, Hong Kong far outpaces much of mainland China in its quality of health care and its standards of living. This is certainly reflected in the region's life expectancy rates: 79 years for men and 86 years for women.

While one must expect that Chinese influence will become greater in the coming years, in the joint declaration in which Britain agreed to return Hong Kong to China, China's leaders promised to respect Hong Kong's existing economic and social structure, as well as its lifestyle. Most residents of the region hope that this will be the case and that Hong Kong will be allowed to continue its economic success. Certainly the region offers a lifestyle with all the activities and pleasures one can find in any modern city in the world.

History and Government

Prior to the British gaining control, Hong Kong was a small fishing community that was home to as many pirates as it was to honest men and women. After being defeated in the Opium War by Britain, China ceded Hong Kong to the British in the Treaty of Nanking in 1842, giving the British Hong Kong in perpetuity. In a later conflict the British added to Hong Kong's size. The Chinese never forgot the loss of this land, however, and in an agreement signed with Britain in December of 1984 were finally promised the return of Hong Kong.

Under British rule, Hong Kong enjoyed laws based on English common law. Now, although China has pledged to respect Hong Kong's existing social and economic systems, it's likely that laws will be changed — if not in actual words certainly in spirit — to reflect Chinese legal precedents. Vestiges of British influence will remain, but Hong Kong will surely assume more of the flavor of the mainland. No one, of course, can predict precisely what will happen in Hong Kong, though most people believe that any change will be gradual. Moreover, it is in China's interest for Hong Kong to remain economically strong and vibrant.

The Economy of Hong Kong

Hong Kong is one of the world's major economic successes. GDP per capita is about U.S. $27,500. The region's free market economy that is burdened with few tariffs continues to move forward. It's likely that as long as China permits Hong Kong to pursue its free market policies the region will prosper.

Hong Kong's infrastructure, as expected with a region that has a bustling economy, is excellent. Modern telecommunications provide superior domestic and international service. Microwave transmissions, satellite links, and undersea cables connect Hong Kong with locations throughout the world. Similarly, air and sea facilities are modern and well equipped.

Much of the economic activity of Hong Kong centers around Victoria, the capital city on Hong Kong Island (Victoria is often referred to as simply Hong Kong) and on the only other major city, Kowloon, on Kowloon Peninsula, which is opposite Victoria. Each city is a cosmopolitan center in its own right.

Hong Kong's financial system is well developed with its banks providing the various services that modern businesses and consumers need and expect. This might change somewhat under Chinese control, although the prospect of

Residence Havens

that is unlikely since the Chinese will prefer Hong Kong to maintain its economic vigor.

Tax Facts of Interest

Note that the following data was valid at the time of this writing. Be sure to check current tax regulations in China and Hong Kong before making any decisions about Hong Kong's status for a retirement haven. Also note, however, that China has pledged to respect Hong Kong's economic system for at least the next 50 years.

Of most interest, <u>residents may receive profits from abroad without incurring tax liability</u>. A Profits Tax, which includes people, corporations, partnerships, trustees and bodies of persons carrying on any trade are chargeable on all profits arising in or derived from Hong Kong.

At the time of this writing, Hong Kong remains an interesting and potentially superior retirement haven. The climate is good, the region enjoys a strong economy, and, despite the Chinese takeover, is likely to maintain its social system, customs, and economic practices. In many respects, Hong Kong is a gateway to the Far East and all that region's wonder. Nevertheless, in considering the overall attractiveness of Hong Kong as a retirement haven, one would be wise to carefully weigh the impact of the Chinese takeover.

Should you wish to learn more about Hong Kong, contact:

U.S. Diplomatic Mission for Hong Kong
Mailing Address: PSC 464, Box 30, FPO AP 96522-0002
Tel: 852-2523-9011
Fax: 852-2845-1598

The Republic of Ireland

Despite the sometimes negative news accounts regarding religious conflict between Protestants and Catholics that Ireland receives, the facts are clear: the Republic of Ireland is poised to become an attractive site for retirement and investment. The island of Ireland is divided into two parts: the Republic of Ireland (which is the focus of this article) and Northern Ireland, which is located at the northern part of the island and is a part of the United Kingdom. It is Northern Ireland that, unfortunately, is the center of much of the violence between Protestants and Catholics that the rest of the world hears about.

The Republic of Ireland comprises the greater part of the island of Ireland, about 27,136 square miles (about 70,280 square kilometers), compared to about 5,500 square miles (about 10,110 square kilometers) for Northern Ireland. In contrast to the east coast which can be characterized as a relatively smooth meeting of sea and land, the island's west coast is known for steep cliffs and numerous islets. Ireland's interior is a mix of small mountain ranges and lowlands.

Ireland's overall climate is somewhat warmer than one would expect to find at its latitude. Indeed, its annual temperatures range about 25 degree F (14 degrees C) warmer in comparison to other places as far north. The reason for the moderation in climate is the Gulf Stream, a great warm water ocean current that starts in the tropics south of the U.S., flows northward and across the Atlantic, a part of it eventually washing against Ireland's western shore. Even after flowing several thousand miles, the warmth of this ocean current is still strong enough to affect the air above Ireland, making it considerably more mild. Average summer temperatures in Ireland generally range between 57 and 68 degrees F (about 14 to 20 degrees C), while average winter temperatures usually fall between 40 and 45 degrees F (about 7 to 14 degrees C). Rainfall averages about 40 inches (100 centimeters) per year.

The Republic of Ireland has a population of 3,700,000. Over a million people live in or around Dublin, the capital city. Most of the population is descended from the Celts, an ancient group of people that inhabited the island, with an English minority. Other ethnic groups are insignificant. The official languages of the country are English and Irish (also known as Gaelic), with English predominating. Most of the population is Roman Catholic, 94%, with 4% being Protestant, and the remaining 2% adhering to other religions.

Ireland's standard of living is very good, comparable to those of the other countries that belong to the EU. The country's literary rate is 99%, and its quality of health care is equal to the health care of other European countries. Life expectancy is 73 years for men and 79 years for women.

Ireland is a beautiful country — considered by many to be one of the most pollution-free of Europe — that offers its residents a variety of pleasures and activities that are found in any modern land. A delightful culture, a sense of history, high spirit, and a superior quality of life make Ireland a potentially excellent retirement haven.

History and Government

Ireland was inhabited prior to 3,500 B.C. by tribes of hunters. The Celts, also known as Gaels, came from the European continent and began settling Ireland about 350 B.C. warring with and replacing the earlier inhabitants. Ireland remained a land of the Celts until the late 700s when Vikings began to raid the coasts. For two hundred years Vikings plundered Ireland, some of the invaders eventually settling and building towns. War between the Vikings and Celts continued for many years.

In the 12th century, the deposed king of Leinster, Dermot MacMurrough, sought aid from the English king to help him regain his throne. This led to the eventual influx of the English, who by 1250 had come to control most of Ireland. Conflict between English and Irish continued on and off for nearly 300 years. When England's King Henry VIII broke with the Roman Catholic Church in 1534, resulting in England becoming a Protestant nation, the troubles between Ireland and England worsened. The conflict continued for centuries, finally being resolved with the Anglo-Irish Treaty in 1921, which essentially freed the counties that would become the Republic of Ireland. The Republic of Ireland became fully free from Great Britain on April 18, 1949. The counties of Northern Island, which had a Protestant majority, preferred to remain a part of Great Britain.

The Republic of Ireland is governed by a constitution which was adopted in 1937. Legislative power resides in a bicameral parliament: the upper chamber is the Senate and the lower chamber is the Dail. The prime minister, who is the actual head of the government, is nominated by the lower house and is appointed by the president. Executive power is held by the prime minister; the president has little real power. Irish laws, as one would expect, are based on English common law.

The Economy of Ireland

In recent years, Ireland's governments have initiated programs that were designed to strengthen and support the country's economy. In particular, policies have been promoted that foster the growth of light industry, tourism, and financial services. Whereas Ireland's economy was once primarily based on agriculture, today agriculture accounts for only about 20% of the country's GNP. Within the past decade or so, Ireland has emerged as a financial services center. This is particularly true of Dublin, which has become a major center for international offshore funds management in Europe.

Ireland's financial services sector is modern and offers a variety of services, including such areas as funds management, asset finance, international banking, and insurance. Its financial system consists of a variety of banks, investment and funds companies, credit companies, and credit unions. The Central Bank of Ireland supervises the financial services industry, and in particular protects the Irish pound, the country's currency.

Ireland's infrastructure is modern and sound. Its telecommunications system is state-of-the-art, its airports are well-equipped, providing service to major cities throughout the world, and its roadways link all parts of the country.

Tax Facts of Interest

Although the tax system in the Republic of Ireland includes an income tax and various other taxes, foreign income (excluding income from the United Kingdom) is not chargeable for non-domiciled residents, except to the extent that such income is remitted to Ireland.

In addition, Ireland offers a variety of tax incentives to encourage foreign investment. Certain manufacturing companies are eligible to benefit from a 10% corporate tax rate. The typical corporate tax rate is 40%. For eligible companies, the 10% rate is available until the year 2010. Certain international financial services companies in Dublin may be eligible for a special 10% tax rate on profits from certified activities, an exemption for 10 years from local property taxes, a 100% write-off for expenditures for new equipment during the first year of operation, a 100% write-off for the costs of new facilities in the first year for owners who occupy their sites, a 54% write-off for new building costs in the first year for lessors, and freedom of withholding tax in the payment of interest to recipients.

The Republic of Ireland

Ireland also has the Shannon Airport Customs Free Zone. Any foreign or domestic company may apply for a license to conduct trading operations in the zone, provided its operations in some way contribute to the development or use of Shannon Airport. <u>Companies granted permission to operate in the Shannon Airport Customs Free Zone are taxed at a rate of 10% through December, 2005</u>.

Those considering retirement might set up a company to take advantage of these significant tax incentives. Once the company has been established, the owner can hand over management to others and enjoy his or her retirement.

Individuals who wish to retire to a land known for its old-fashioned values, picturesque scenery, and stability would do well to consider Ireland. Should you wish to find out more about the Republic of Ireland, contact:

The Irish Tourist Board
Baggot Street Bridge
Dublin 8
Ireland
Tel: +353-1-602-4000
Fax: +353-1-602-4000

Note: The U.S. Office of the Irish Tourist Board may be reached by calling 800-223-6470.

The United States Embassy in Ireland
42 Elgin Road, Ballsbridge
Dublin
Ireland
Tel: +353-1-668-8777

The Industrial Development Authority in Ireland
Wilton Park House
Wilton Place, Dublin 2
Dublin
Ireland
Tel: 01-668-6633
Fax: 01-660-3703

The Industrial Development Authority — New York
17th Floor, 345 Park Ave.
New York, NY 10154
Tel: 212-750-4300
Fax: 212-750-7357

The Industrial Development Authority — Japan
Room 1205
Kioicho TBR Building
7 Kojimachi 5-Chrome
Chiyoda-Ku, Tokyo 102
Japan
Tel: 3-3262-7621
Fax: 3-3261-4239

The Industrial Development Authority — Sydney
Level 5
36 Carrington St.
GPO 4909, Sydney
New South Wales 2000
Tel: 2-262-2873
Fax: 2-262-2913

Israel

Despite newspaper reports that highlight violence between Israeli and Arab militants, Israel and its neighboring Arab countries, during the last few years, have taken important steps toward achieving a lasting peace in the region. Peace throughout the Middle East will only enhance Israel's potential as a retirement haven.

Israel is a small country, about the size of New Jersey, with an area of 7,992 square miles (about 20,700 square kilometers). A land of low hills and plains, Israel borders the Mediterranean Sea on the west, while to the north lies Lebanon, to the east is Jordon, and to the southwest is Egypt.

Israel has a subtropical climate with wide extremes, depending on location. Although many people unfamiliar with the country assume that it is mostly desert (based on an assumption that most of the Middle East is excessively dry), Israel's rainfall varies with locality and time of the year. In the Upper Galilee in the north, average annual rainfall is about 32 inches (80 centimeters), while in the south in a region known as the Negev, rainfall averages less than 2 inches (about 3.5 centimeters) per year. This area is desert. Average annual temperatures likewise vary from 40 degrees F (5 degrees C) in winter to 95 degrees F (35 degrees C) in summer. Overall, April to October are generally hot and humid with less rain, while November to March are cooler with increased amounts of precipitation.

Israel's slightly more than 5,000,000 people are predominately Jewish, 83%, with the rest of the population being mostly Arab. The major religions of the country are Judaism, to which almost all of the Jewish population adheres, Muslim, 14%, with the remainder being Christian and belonging to other minority faiths. Hebrew and Arabic are the official languages, but English is widely spoken.

The quality of Israel's standard of living is high. The country's literacy rate is 92% (although of the Arab population, this falls to 70%), and its health care is on a par with advanced countries throughout the world. Life expectancy rates are 76 years for men and 80 years for women.

History and Government

Israel's long history is interwoven with violence. The land has been fought over for thousands of years. It is thought that Judaism was established as a religion during the time of King David and his successors between the years 1000 B.C. to 600 B.C., after which Israel was invaded by Babylonians, Persians, and Greeks. For a time in the second century B.C. Israel regained its independence, only to see the Romans arrive and establish domination.

Arab invaders gained control of Israel in 636 and remained in control for hundreds of years, in time giving way to Seljuks, Mamluks, Christian Crusaders, and Ottomans. Israel did not fully regain its independence until after World War II, through a resolution of the United Nations in 1948. Its independence, however, angered Arab states, and resulted in several wars. Finally, in the 1990s, genuine peace talks began, and in 1993 a historic agreement was signed between Israel and the Palestine Liberation Organization (PLO). The road to peace continues today.

Israel's government is a parliamentary democracy. Legislative power resides with Israel's parliament, the Knesset. The Knesset elects a president for a five-year term, but he has little actual power. A prime minister, who is elected separately, is the real head of the government. Israel's judiciary has two parts — a civil system and a religious system. The civil system deals with cases of a criminal or civil nature, while the religious system handles court cases that have to do with marriage, divorce, alimony, and wills.

The Economy of Israel

Because of its great need to defend itself in face of hostile neighbors, Israel's economy has evolved to be a mix of private enterprise and government controlled industries and services. Government control focuses mostly on industries that support the country's infrastructure such as electricity, water supplies, telecommunications, railways and airports. The bulk of Israel's industrial goods, however, are produced by private companies.

Overall, Israel's economy is diversified and rather strong. It is likely that the country's economy will grow, in great part because of the expanding demand for consumer goods throughout the Middle East.

Israel has an excellent infrastructure. Its telecommunications systems are advanced and its systems of transportation are modern and efficient. Israel's infrastructure is by far the best in the region.

The country's financial system is also modern. Banking and investment services are equal to any of those found in other advanced countries. The country's monetary unit is the New Sheqalim.

Tax Facts of Interest

Over the years, as a necessity to fund a high defense budget, Israelis have been burdened with an assortment of taxes. Income tax, for example, includes income from numerous sources, and rates are progressive, rising to 50%. However, there are some significant exemptions (either partially or totally), including exemptions that apply to:

- <u>Certain handicapped individuals.</u>
- <u>Victims of hostile action or Nazi persecution.</u>
- <u>Dependents of deceased members of fighting services in respect of pensions payable by government.</u>
- <u>Temporary residents in respect of income derived from sources abroad, provided the individual has not lived in Israel for more than six months in the year preceding of assessment and the individual does not intend to stay permanently.</u>
- <u>New residents in respect of income received from abroad for the first seven years of residence.</u>
- <u>Nonresidents in respect of interest on certain types of securities and loans.</u>

In addition:

- <u>There is no tax on foreign-source income for the first 30 years for a new immigrant.</u> This exemption is especially attractive to an individual who has investments or pension income from outside of Israel.
- <u>Taxable income may be adjusted for inflation.</u>
- <u>Exemptions are possible for taxes on capital gains derived from securities found on the Tel Aviv Stock Exchange.</u>

Israel also has signed double-taxation agreements with several countries that investors and retired individuals may find beneficial.

In an effort to encourage investment from both domestic and foreign sources, the Israeli government has passed legislation that offers generous tax incentives. For entrepreneurs who might consider beginning a company in Israel and then retiring, these incentives may be of interest.

Israel

Any company that is an *Approved Enterprise* is eligible for incentives, which include the following:

- Reduced tax rates to as low as 10% for a period of ten years.

- Grants of up to 38% of the cost of fixed assets. If the right to receive grants is waived, a full tax exemption for up to 10 years may be obtained.

- Accelerated schedules for depreciation of equipment.

In addition, the Israeli government has established free zones to foster the country's economy. A business conducting its operations from within a free zone may be entitled to the following incentives:

- In the Eilat Free Trade Zone, an exemption from value added tax, refunds of up to 20% on gross wages paid to employees; individuals residing in Eilat may receive tax credits of up to 10% of their taxable income that is obtained from employment or business conducted in Eilat.

- In the Free Port Zones of Eilat, Ashdod, and Haifa, an exemption from all income taxes for seven years and a maximum tax rate of 30% after the seven-year period, a tax of 15% of dividends derived from income, an exemption from property taxes, and in some cases, an exemption from capital gains tax for shareholders.

Should you wish to find out more about Israel, contact:

The Israel Government Tourist Office
800 Second Ave.
New York, NY 10017
Tel: 212-499-5650, 5645 or 800-596-1199
Fax: 212-499-5655

Residence Havens

*The Israel Government Tourist Office
24 King George St.
Jerusalem
Israel
Tel: +972-2-75-48-63*

*The Minister of Economic Affairs
Embassy of Israel
3514 International Dr., NW
Washington, DC 20008
Tel: 202-364-5692
Fax: 202-364-5647*

Jordan

Jordan is a small Arab nation that occupies an important location in the Middle East. It is bordered on the north by Syria, on the east by Iraq and Saudi Arabia, on the south by Saudi Arabia and the Gulf of Aqaba, and on the west by Israel. Having an area of 37,738 square miles (97,740 square kilometers), Jordan is slightly smaller than the state of Indiana.

Jordan is, for the most part, an arid plateau that reaches an elevation of between 2,000 and 3,000 feet (about 600 to 900 meters). Jordan's climate is best described as dry, however, a rainy season occurs in the western part of the country from November to April. Even here, though, annual average rainfall amounts seldom exceed 26 inches (about 66 centimeters). In the eastern part of the country, an annual rainfall total of less than 5 inches (about 13 centimeters) is not uncommon. Temperatures vary rather distinctly with location. In the Jordan valley, for example, summer temperatures may reach 120 degrees F (49 degrees C), while in Amman, the capital city, the average summer temperature is 78 degrees F (26 degrees C). The country's average winter temperature is about 45 degrees F (7 degrees C), although subfreezing temperatures may be experienced in some areas in January.

Jordan's population is slightly more than 4,200,000. About 98% of the country's people are Arab, with 1% being Circassian, and the other 1% being Armenian. About 92% of Jordanians are Sunni Muslim with the remaining 8% being Christian. Arab is the nation's official language, although English is widely understood among the country's upper and middle classes and is spoken in many parts of the country. Throughout Jordan the signs of many businesses and road signs are in English as well as Arabic. About 86% of the country's people are literate.

Jordan offers its people a high standard of living. Health care is good, particularly in and around Amman, and life expectancy rates are high: 71 years for men and 75 years for women. Various recreational activities and cultural events — including art exhibits, lectures, and concerts — are available as is choice housing. Supermarkets and shops carry a wide variety of products that are common in American and European homes. Numerous fine restaurants, offering an assortment of excellent international dishes, are located in Amman.

In recent years Jordan has enacted legislation to encourage international businesses to locate regional headquarters in the country. This is part of an initiative to strengthen the country's economy and take advantage of the expanding markets in the Middle East. Jordan clearly wishes to become a major regional headquarters center. One of the results of this is to open Jordan to the world.

Jordan's economy is based more firmly in principles of capitalism than other countries of the region. Moreover, the nation has a good record of economic stability, a high standard of living, and quality system of education. Understanding the requirements for entry into the global economy, Jordan has made English a mandatory subject in the nation's schools. The country has the potential to be an excellent retirement haven.

History and Government

In ancient times, Jordan was the site of some of the world's earliest civilizations. Some of these — the Ammonites and the Kingdoms of Edom, Gilead, and Moab — are mentioned in the Bible. At one time or another, the land that became Jordan was controlled by the Egyptians, Assyrians, Babylonians, Persians, and Romans. After the Romans, the Byzantines controlled Jordan, losing control to the Arabs between 633 and 636. Christians controlled parts of Jordan during the Crusades, and from 1517 to 1918 Jordan was governed by the Ottoman Turks.

After World War I, Great Britain was awarded Jordan and the land of Israel through a mandate of the League of Nations. In 1922, the British divided the mandate into two parts, Palestine and Transjordan. Transjordan obtained qualified independence from Britain through a treaty in 1928. In 1946, the British relinquished their mandate over Transjordan, an act that led to the independence of the modern country of Jordan. Also after the war, the nation of Israel was created, which led to rising tensions in the Middle East.

By 1948, together with the forces of other Arab nations, Transjordan was at war with Israel. This was only the beginning of years of periodic warfare and violence throughout the region. In 1950 Transjordan merged with Arab-held Palestine, and the prefix "Trans" was officially dropped from Jordan's name.

In recent years, Jordanians have come to see peace as a requirement to economic growth and stability throughout the region. Jordan has negotiated a peace treaty with Israel that has established diplomatic relations and allowed for economic cooperation and security between the two countries.

Modern Jordan is a constitutional monarchy with a bicameral legislature. The chief of state is the king, while the head of the government is the prime minister. The cabinet is appointed by the king, who wields much of the nation's power. The National Assembly consists of the House of Notables, a 40-member body appointed by the king, and the House of Representatives, whose members are elected. Suffrage is universal for citizens 20 years of age and older. The country's laws are based on Islamic law and French codes.

The Economy of Jordan

Although Jordan is striving to strengthen its economy, the country struggles with inadequate supplies of water and natural resources. The country is also burdened with a high debt, poverty, and unemployment.

The economy centers around a few important industries and agriculture. Phosphate mining, cement, light manufacturing, and petroleum refining (unlike many of its neighbors, Jordan has little oil reserves) constitute the bulk of the nation's industry. Agriculture focuses on grains, olives, vegetables, and fruits. About 20% of the country's labor force works at manufacturing and mining, and another 20% at agriculture. Much of the rest works in the service sector. Underemployment is an on-going concern among many workers, and per capita GDP is not much more than U.S. $1,000.

Jordan's infrastructure is generally considered to be good. Phone service is dependable within cities, with direct dialing to most countries. The telecommunications system is constantly being modernized and expanded. Although Jordan's seaports need to be expanded and updated, the country's airports are adequate and its roadways are good.

The financial system in Jordan is also considered to be good. Various commercial and foreign banks offer numerous services for consumers and businesses. While banks in Amman and Aqaba offer cash advances on major credit cards, credit cards are not usually accepted outside the larger hotels and businesses. U.S. dollars, though, are accepted in most places. The nation's monetary unit is the Dinar.

Tax Facts of Interest

While there are few tax exemptions available to individuals, Jordan offers considerable incentives to businesses. Under the Foreign Companies Registration Law, a foreign company can establish a Jordan-based branch for conducting business outside of Jordan. While sales to domestic markets are not permitted, the vast market of the rest of the Middle East provides an abundant potential customer base.

Companies that register under the Foreign Companies Registration Law are eligible for several significant tax benefits, including:

- Total exemption from income taxes.
- Total exemption from social security taxes.
- Exemption from the payment of business registration taxes.
- Exemption from registrations with the Chamber of Commerce.
- Exemptions from customs duties on the furnishings and equipment for the Jordanian branch office.
- Exemptions from duties on the importation of commercial samples.

In addition, non-Jordanian employees of the Jordan-based regional office are eligible for various incentives, including:

- An exemption from income and social security taxes.
- An exemption on customs duties on household furniture.
- Duty-free importation of a car every two years.
- The availability of residential and work permits.

Residence Havens

These exemptions make Jordan an attractive haven for individuals who might wish to start a branch office of their company in Jordan, and work at the business and prosper from the generous tax benefits. Of course, after establishing the business, they may then retire and continue to profit from the advantageous tax laws the company is subject to.

Should you wish to find out more information about Jordan, contact the following:

The Embassy of Jordan
3504 International Drive, NW
Washington, DC 20008
Tel: 202-966-2664
Fax: 202-966-3110

U.S. Diplomatic Mission in Jordan
P.O. Box 354
Amman 11118 Jordan
APO AE 09892-0200
Tel: 962-6-820101
Fax: 962-6-820159

In addition, here are some helpful phone numbers in Jordan:

The Ministry of Tourism and Antiquities: 962-6-642311
Irbid Tourist Office: 962-2-241744
Ramtha Tourist Office: 962-2-283074
Madaba Tourist Office: 962-8-543376

Malta

Malta is located between Italy and North Africa in the center of the Mediterranean Sea. It is an independent republic in the Commonwealth of Nations. Usually thought of as being a single island, Malta is a group of islands, including Malta, the principal island, Gozo, Comino, Cominotto, and Filfla.

The island group has an area of about 122 square miles (316 square kilometers) with the island of Malta having the largest share, about 95 square miles (246 square kilometers). The other islands that make up the group are smaller. The Maltese islands are relatively low, with the highest point being about 785 feet (239 meters) in elevation, and have irregular coastlines.

Malta's climate is quite nice. Average temperatures range from about 89 degrees F (32 degrees C) in summer to 57 degrees F (15 degrees C) in winter. The islands are rather dry, averaging about 22 inches (56 centimeters) of rainfall per year. Sunshine is abundant.

Malta has a population of about 370,000 people, whose ethnic origins represent many of the lands around the Mediterranean and Europe. Throughout history the islands have been a crossroads to destinations throughout the Mediterranean and the population reflects roots that can be traced back to the Phoenicians, Carthaginians, Romans, Byzantines, Arabs, Normans, French, and British. Because of its history, Malta has evolved into a truly diverse and unique culture.

This wonderful culture is apparent in the historical language of the Maltese people, which, although of Semitic origin, is built on an alphabet and grammar derived from Latin. In addition to Maltese, English is an official language and the language of business, however, Italian is also spoken by many residents.

Residence Havens

Indeed, much of the population is multi-lingual. Although the predominate religion is Roman Catholicism, other religions are well represented.

The overall standard of living on Malta is excellent. Both private and public health care facilities are comparable to those of Great Britain, and virtually all of the population has access to health care. Life expectancy is 75 years for men and 79 years for women. Education is valued on Malta, as evidenced by the literacy rate of 90%, and the fact that education on all levels is free. The University of Malta was established in 1592 and continues to provide quality advanced learning and scholarship.

Malta offers a superior lifestyle in virtually all respects. The islands are clean and picturesque. Malta offers attractive housing, fine restaurants and nightclubs, and numerous recreational activities. Golf, tennis, swimming, and sailing are quite popular. Residents and visitors can enjoy the casino in St. Julians, as well as Malta's beaches, which are renowned for their beauty.

When combined with a variety of special tax exemptions that the Maltese government offers, these features make Malta one of the world's most attractive retirement havens.

History and Government

Evidence suggests that the islands of Malta were inhabited as early as 4000 B.C. Around 1000 B.C. the islands became a Phoenician colony, used by those ancient seafarers as a stopover point as they traded throughout the Mediterranean. The Greeks took control of the islands in 736 B.C., eventually losing control to the Carthaginians, who in turn lost the islands to the Romans. When the Romans divided their empire in 395, Malta was officially placed under the control of the Eastern Empire, which subsequently came to be the Byzantine Empire. For much of the next 400 years, Malta remained under the rule of the Byzantines. In 870, however, the Arabs seized the islands and remained in control until 1090 when they were conquered by a Norman army. After this, Malta passed to the control of the Kingdom of Sicily.

In the following years, Malta was controlled by the Holy Roman Empire, the Knights of Saint John of Jerusalem, Napoleon, and Great Britain. The British administered Malta as a colony for over 150 years, granting the islands independence in 1964. It was during these years that the English traditions of democracy were established.

Malta today is a parliamentary democracy. The head of state is the president, who is appointed by the parliament to serve a five-year term. The actual head of government, however, is the prime minister, who is appointed by the president from among the members of the parliament. Legislative authority resides in the House of Representatives, whose 65 members are elected for five-year terms via universal suffrage. Malta's laws are based mostly on British common law.

The Economy of Malta

Malta has a robust economy, which has grown and diversified in recent years. In the past, Malta's economy was based largely on agriculture; today major industries include machinery, textiles, high-tech products (especially electronics), and food and beverages. Tourism is a rapidly growing sector of the economy, and Malta has also become a vital center for international financial services.

Malta's infrastructure is efficient and modern. The islands' sea- and airports, roadways, and telecommunications are continually being upgraded to support the country's economy. Malta's seaports, for example, possess some of the Mediterranean's most modern equipment and provide efficient service to most major European and Mediterranean ports. Malta's airports host numerous international carriers and provide quality service to destinations around the world. The telecommunications system is likewise equal to some of the best in the world. Malta has direct satellite links, a digital exchange, and fiber optic network that provides reliable service with over 100 countries. A mobile phone network is also available.

Along with an excellent infrastructure, Malta's financial system is capable of meeting the needs of any business or consumer. As an important international center for financial services, Malta's financial system is flexible and efficient. Numerous banks and financial institutions provide the services and products that consumers and entrepreneurs throughout the modern world expect and require. The country's currency is the Maltese Lira. Malta's Central Bank is given the responsibility for ensuring the stability of the islands' currency.

Tax Facts of Interest

Malta's tax code is designed to promote investment in Malta and the retention of Maltese wealth. There are various exemptions and incentives that might be attractive to individuals seeking a retirement haven.

<u>There are no property taxes, real estate taxes, municipal or local taxes in Malta. Income and capital gains arising outside of Malta are subject to tax only if the recipient is both domiciled and a resident of Malta. Expatriates are not required to pay capital gains tax, and foreign residents are taxed only a small percentage on the amount they bring into the country for living expenses. In addition, Malta also has signed double-taxation treaties with several countries.</u>

The Maltese government has also enacted legislation that provides for significant tax incentives for investors and businesses, including:

- Industries that are at least 95% export-oriented may receive a tax holiday of ten years.

- Special investment tax credits.

- Accelerated allowances for depreciation.

- Reduced rates for reinvested profits.

- When used in export products, duty-free importation of parts or materials.

- Duty-free shipment on various products shipped to the EC.

- Reduced tariffs on products exported to the U.S.

The island of Malta has an excellent climate, a high standard of living, and offers several important tax incentives. Should you be interested in finding out more about Malta as a possible retirement haven, contact:

The Embassy of Malta
2017 Connecticut Ave., NW
Washington, DC 20008
Tel: 202-462-3611
Fax: 202-387-5470

Malta Development Corporation
House of Catalunya
Marsamxetto Rd.
P.O. Box 571
Valletta, Malta
Tel: 356-221523
Fax: 356-246408

Mexico

Mexico is located in Middle America, south of the U.S. and north of Belize and Guatemala. To the east Mexico's shores are touched by the Caribbean Sea, while its western shores meet the Pacific Ocean.

Mexico is a rather large country, slightly less than three times the size of Texas, and extends much longer north to south than it is wide east to west. The country has an area of 761,604 square miles (1,972,550 square kilometers). Its topography includes high, rugged mountains, high plateaus, desert, and low coastal lands. Although the country's highest point is Volcan Pico de Orizaba at 18,240 feet (5,700 meters), the most distinctive topographical feature of Mexico is the Central Plateau, for which the elevation in places ranges between 5,000 and 8,000 feet (1,500 to 2,440 meters). Mexico City, the nation's capital, is located on the Central Plateau.

Because of the country's north-south length, and also its changing elevation, Mexico's climate varies from tropical to desert depending on location, affected most by altitude. In the low coastal plains, the weather is generally humid, with temperatures ranging from 60 to 120 degrees F (15.6 to 49 degrees C). Southern coastal regions, particularly the Yucatan Peninsula, tend to be tropical. Between elevations of 3,000 to 6,000 feet (1,830 to 2,745 meters) the average temperatures range from 62 to 70 degrees F (16.7 to 21.1 degrees C), while between 6,000 to 9,000 feet the average temperatures vary from 59 to 63 degrees F (15 to 17.2 degrees C). While parts of southern Mexico receive abundant annual rainfall, from 39 to 118 inches (99 to 300 centimeters), much of Mexico is dry. Parts of the northwest are desert.

Mexico's population of 95,772,400 is growing rapidly. Indeed, the rapidly increasing population has brought with it a host of problems such as poverty, unemployment and underemployment. About 60% of Mexicans are Mestizos, with Amerindians comprising about 30% of the population and Caucasians

9%. The rest of the population is composed of small numbers of other groups. Spanish is the official language, however, various Mayan dialects are also spoken. Mexico's literacy rate is close to 90%. About 90% of Mexico's people are Roman Catholics, with most of the remainder belonging to Protestant faiths.

Mexico is a country of both great wealth and deep poverty. Parts of Mexico City, the nation's capital, rival any modern cosmopolitan center in the world, even as other parts are equal to some of the world's worst slums. Acapulco is a world-class resort, yet residents of some villages in remote areas live in primitive conditions. Good health care is available in the major cities, but its access diminishes in outlying areas. Life expectancy is 70 years for men and 77 for women.

In recent years Mexico has become a prime tourist destination. It is a vast country that has activities and pleasures for just about everyone. Mexico possesses marvelous luxury resorts, hundreds of miles of beautiful beaches, charming colonial towns, and a culture and history that visitors and new residents can spend leisurely hours exploring. Without question, many of Mexico's visitor are drawn by its culture, which is a mix of Spanish, Indian, and American traditions. There are few places in the world like Mexico. For thousands of people, many from the U.S., Mexico has become a retirement haven.

History and Government

Mexico was the home to some of the earliest and most advanced civilizations in the New World. Several Indian civilizations, most notably the Mayans, Toltecs, and Aztecs, controlled parts of Mexico through its history prior to the arrival of the Spanish. It was the Aztec Empire that the Spanish Conquistador Hernando Cortez encountered in 1519 and soon defeated, making Mexico a Spanish colony. After three hundred years of Spanish rule,

Mexicans rebelled and after years of fighting finally won their independence, declaring Mexico a republic in 1823.

Mexico's history through the 19th century was stormy, highlighted by civil wars, dictators, and wars with Texas, the U.S., and France. Several leaders tried to address the country's uneven distribution of wealth, but, except for minor changes, most failed. After much fighting by rival forces against the dictatorial rule of Porfirio Diaz, a new constitution was adopted on Feb. 5, 1917. The new constitution provided for social reform, and since its adoption Mexican governments have developed large-scale social programs.

Mexico is a federal republic. Citizens 18 years of age and older have the right to vote. The chief of state and head of the government is the president, who is elected for a six-year term. The legislative branch of the government is a bicameral National Congress composed of a Senate and Chamber of Deputies. The country's legal system is based on U.S. constitutional theory and a civil law system.

The Economy of Mexico

Mexico has a free market economy in which the private sector is growing in importance and influence. In the mid-1990s Mexico suffered through one of its worst recessions since the 1930s, however, since then the country's economy has slowly expanded. Nevertheless, Mexico's economy continues to struggle with some serious weaknesses, including relatively high unemployment with substantial underemployment, a vulnerable financial system, and dissension among the country's leaders on which course would be most beneficial for the nation. The per capita GDP is just under $8,000, but purchasing power is eroded by a persistent high rate of inflation.

On the other hand, there is reason for optimism regarding Mexico's economy. The country possesses much mineral wealth in silver, lead, zinc,

Residence Havens

gold, oil, and natural gas. The industrial sector of the economy, which makes up about 30% of the country's total, includes such enterprises as chemicals, iron and steel, petroleum, mining, food and beverages, textiles, clothing, and motor vehicles. Tourism has been and continues to be a vital sector of the economy.

Mexico's infrastructure is, for the most part, sound and efficient, particularly in the cities. The telecommunications system is highly developed with extensive microwave radio relay links. Although the service provided to the government and businesses is very good, service to the general population, especially as one moves away from the cities, is often inadequate. Mexico has numerous sea- and airports. Those located within the major cities are efficient and modern. Highways that connect major cities are good, however, many remote small towns and villages are connected with unpaved roadways.

While Mexico's banks and financial institutions offer the many services and products that consumers and businesses expect in any modern, developed country, some international banking authorities regard its overall financial system with caution. In 1994, for example, Mexico was forced to devalue the peso, which led to a contraction of economic activity by about 7%. Most investors well remember the controversy that resulted when President Clinton moved to ensure Mexico's financial health by pledging the support of American dollars.

Tax Facts of Interest

Mexico has few tax incentives for individuals, however, the tax code provides some important benefits for people living in Mexico on a semi-permanent basis and also those residents who gain their income from writing and music.

Tourists in Mexico are not taxable residents. Since a tourist card is good for six months per trip, many people live in Mexico on a semi-permanent basis

130

Mexico

by leaving the country for one day every six months. Thus, they are not subject to tax.

Income gained from royalties obtained from copyrights on literary, artistic or scientific works, and also including such productions as films, radio and TV recordings, are taxed at a rate of 15%, which is considerably less than the standard rates.

Some tax incentives are also available for certain assembly plants. Assembly plants engaged primarily in export may be eligible for duty-free importation of goods for assembly and finishing.

Mexico also has free zones. Industries located in the free zones may import materials and goods duty-free.

Some companies would undoubtedly find these to be major benefits, and entrepreneus who are considering the establishment of a business and eventual retirement would be wise to consider the opportunity these incentives provide.

Although Mexico has its share of problems, it is unquestionably a beautiful land with a long and fascinating history. Parts of Mexico are like a tropical paradise, and it is for this reason that many people — especially Americans — move to Mexico for retirement.

Should you be interested in finding out more about retiring to Mexico, contact:

The Mexican Government Tourist Office
405 Park Ave., Suite 1401
New York, NY 10022
Tel. 800-446-3942

The Mexican Government Tourist Office
181 University Ave., Suite 1112
Toronto M5H 3M7
Canada
Tel: 800-263-9426

The Mexican Embassy
1911 Pennsylvania Ave., NW
Washington, DC 20006
Tel: 202-728-1600

U.S. Diplomatic Mission to Mexico
Paseo de la Reforma 305
Colonia Cuauhtemoc
06500 Mexico, Distrito Federal
Mailing Address: P.O. Box 3087
Laredo, TX 78044-3087
Tel: 52-5-211-0042
Fax: 52-5-511-9980, 208-3373

Monaco

Monaco is a small independent principality of Europe. An enclave of southeastern France, it is surrounded on the west, north, and east by France, and is bordered by the Mediterranean Sea on the south.

A famous resort, Monaco is only 0.7 square miles (1.8 square kilometers) in area. The principality is divided into five areas: Monaco, the capital, La Condamine, or the harbor area, Monte Carlo, known best for its casino, Fontvieille, and Moneghetti.

The residents of Monaco enjoy a nice climate that is mild in winter and warm in summer. Average temperatures in January and February are about 46 degrees F (8 degrees C), while temperatures in July and August average 77 degrees F (25 degrees C). Sunshine is abundant throughout the year.

Monaco has a population of about 30,000 people. Of these, some 12,000 are French, 5,000 are Italian, and 5,000 are Monegasques. The rest of the population is comprised mostly of other Europeans. Roman Catholicism is the religion of the state, however, freedom of religion is guaranteed by the constitution.

Although many people believe that Monaco is home to the wealthiest of the wealthy — and certainly in some cases this is true — a nice apartment with a seaview will run about U.S.$1,000 per month, which is considerably less than even mediocre apartments in some of the world's big cities.

The official language of Monaco is French, however, many of the principality's people converse in Monegasque, a mixture of French and Italian. English is also spoken and understood by many of the residents.

Residence Havens

Along with being a major resort with an exceptionally delightful lifestyle, superior beaches, golf and tennis clubs, sailing, and gambling, Monaco is close to the great cities of Europe. It can be a wonderful retirement haven.

History and Government

Monaco has been inhabited since ancient times. The name Monaco, for example, likely comes from the Ligurian tribe of the Monoikos, who occupied the site in the sixth century B.C.

Monaco's recorded history begins in the 13th century A.D. when rival families in Italy struggled for power. In 1297, the house of Grimaldi, a Genoese family, seized the fortress that had been built on the spot on which the present Prince's palace stands. The Grimaldis retained possession until 1793 when the principality was annexed by France. In 1815, as one of the results of the Treaty of Vienna, Monaco was made a protectorate of the kingdom of Sardinia. In 1861, Monaco became an independent state under the guardianship of France, and in 1911 it was granted a constitution by Prince Albert I. With this constitution, Monaco was no longer an absolute monarchy. The constitution was modified in 1917, 1933, and once again in 1962. The constitution of 1962 reduced the power of the sovereign, creating a system in which power is shared by the Prince and the National Council of 18 members. Council members are elected by universal suffrage for five-year terms. Much of Monaco's laws are based on French laws.

The Economy of Monaco

While tourism remains an important part of Monaco's economy, economic activity also centers around banking and insurance, pharmaceuticals, electronic equipment, and cosmetics. A major source of revenue is the gambling casino at Monte Carlo.

The principality's financial system is comprised of some of the world's major banks. American Express, Citibank, Chase, Credit Suisse, Grindlays, and NatWest are all represented, offering services that cater to the ordinary consumer up to the truly wealthy. The main currency is the French franc.

As would be expected with the principality being a major tourist site, Monaco's infrastructure is excellent.

Tax Facts of Interest

<u>Monaco has no personal income tax</u> (except for French nationals under specific conditions). In addition Monaco offers significant advantages in the administration of mutual funds. <u>Based on legislation introduced in 1988, neither the Monegasque fund, nor its investors, are subject to income tax or capital gains tax in Monaco. Also, investors may find that Monaco is an excellent place for locally tax-free administration of closely-held investment trusts.</u>

Should you be interested in finding out more information about Monaco, contact:

Monaco Government Tourist and Convention Bureau
845 Third Ave.
New York, NY 10022
Tel: 212-759-5227
Fax: 212-754-9320

Direction du Tourisme et des Congress de la Principaute de Monaco
2a Boulevard des Moulins
MC 98030 Monaco Cedex
Tel: 92-16-61-16
Fax: 92-16-60-00

Monaco Government Tourist and Convention Office
3/8 Chelsea Garden Market
Chelsea Harbour
London SW10 0XE
England
Tel: 71-352-9962
Fax: 71-352-2103

Monaco Touristik-Information
Rosenstrasse 10 — P.O. Box 3201 31
D-4000 Dusseldorf 30 (BRD)
Tel: 211-49-38-92
Fax: 211-49-73-194

Monaco-Seiku-Kanko-Kyoku
Hibiya Kokusai Bld.
11F — 2-3 Uchiasaiwai-Cho 2 Chome
Chiyoda-Ku, Tokyo 100
Japan
Tel: 03-501-2808
Fax: 03-501-2819

Nicaragua

Nicaragua is the largest country of Central America. It is bordered on the north by Honduras, on the east by the Caribbean Sea, on the south by Costa Rica, and on the west by the Pacific Ocean. Slightly larger than New York State, Nicaragua has an area of 50,193 square miles (about 130,000 square kilometers).

Like most Central American countries, Nicaragua has coastal lowlands rising to interior mountains that run roughly north to south through the country. Volcanoes dot the Pacific coastal plain. Some of Nicaragua's mountains approach elevations of 6,900 feet (about 2,100 meters) with the highest point being Mogoton at 7,800 feet (2,438 meters). In the eastern part of the country, the coastal plain, known as the Mosquito Coast, extends about 45 miles inland (about 72 kilometers).

Nicaragua's climate varies with elevation. Coastal regions are tropical, while the highlands and mountains are cooler. In the lowlands, the mean average temperature is about 78 degrees F (about 26 degrees C); in the higher elevations average temperatures vary between 60 and 80 degrees F (about 15 and 27 degrees C). A rainy season extends from May to October, with rainfall being heaviest along the Caribbean coast which may receive 150 inches (380 centimeters) of rain per year.

About 4,300,000 people live in Nicaragua. Of the population, 69% are Mestizos, 17% are of European descent, 9% are black, and 5% are descended from Indians. Close to 90% of Nicaraguans are Roman Catholics with most of the rest belonging to Protestant denominations. Spanish is the country's official language, however, English and Indian languages are also spoken. The literacy rate is about 65%.

Except for life in the major cities — most notably Managua, the capital, and Leon — the standard of living in much of Nicaragua is not up the levels of the U.S., Western Europe, and leading countries of Asia. While health care is adequate in the cities, its availability and quality decline rapidly in outlying areas.

Despite the poverty that is found throughout much of Nicaragua, the country does offer various activities for visitors. Sightseeing at archeological sites, volcanoes, and museums, hiking, fishing, and surfing are all popular attractions. Numerous restaurants offer good meals priced between U.S.$5-$10, and reggae clubs offer relaxation and dancing. Residential areas offer fine housing and guesthouses.

History and Government

Prior to the arrival of the Spanish in 1552, Nicaragua was inhabited by various Indian tribes. From 1552 until 1821 when it achieved independence from Spain, the land was a Spanish colony. For a short period thereafter, Nicaragua was united with Mexico, then with the United Provinces of Central America, becoming an independent republic in 1838. Democratic rule, however, was never fully established, and the country suffered internal strife well into the 20th century. The U.S. sent marines to Nicaragua to quell disturbances during some of the most difficult periods, the last time being 1926 to 1933.

In the latter part of the 20th century, Nicaragua, for a time, regularly appeared in U.S. news broadcasts that highlighted the overthrow of the Somoza regime and the following conflict between the Sandinistas and the Contras. The civil war, along with governmental mismanagement, devastated the country's economy, which only in recent years has begun to recover.

Nicaragua is a republic with its capital at Managua. The chief of state is the president, who is elected for a five-year term by universal suffrage of citizens 16 years of age and older. The legislative branch of the government resides in the National Assembly, and the country's judicial system has been developed on a code of civil laws. The current government is based on a constitution adopted in 1987.

Arising from the strife and turmoil of the 1980s was a host of political parties and pressure groups, many of which espouse radically different agendas. As a result, the country is frequently governed through coalitions of these various elements.

The Economy of Nicaragua

During the civil war of the 1980s, Nicaragua's economy was decimated, and has only begun to rebound in the last few years. A major reason for current economic growth was the government's initiation of a economic stabilization program in the early 1990s. This has led to an impressive reduction in inflation and the obtaining of substantial aid from abroad. From 1991 to 1992, the inflation rate fell from 750% to less than 5%. Although the rate has fluctuated somewhat since then, it has generally averaged about 10%. Similarly, economic output has increased, mostly because of a surge in exports.

Several key sectors comprise Nicaragua's economy. Some of its important industries include: chemicals, textiles, metal products, oil refining, and food processing. Chief crops include bananas, cotton, fruit, yucca, coffee, sugar, corn, cocoa, rice, and tobacco. The country also has mineral deposits of gold, silver, copper, and tungsten.

In recent years, the GDP growth rate has averaged about 4%, while the GDP per capita is slightly under U.S.$1,800. The country's unemployment rate is high, averaging about 20%, but this doesn't account for the substantial underemployment.

While clearly there is potential for continued economic growth in Nicaragua, the country's infrastructure must be modernized. The telephone system is being expanded, but, except for the major cities, is unable to meet the needs of most Nicaraguans. According to some estimates, there is one phone for every 80 people. Roads, particularly outside the cities may be unpaved or riddled with holes and ruts. It's estimated that less than 25% of the country's roads are paved. Sea- and airports provide service, but hardly what can be found in other parts of the world. To its credit, the government is attempting to modernize the nation's infrastructure, but major improvement is unlikely any time soon.

Nicaragua's financial system, while offering the various services that businesses and consumers in most modern countries expect, is somewhat suspect for its overall strength and stability. The Cordoba is the country's currency.

Tax Facts of Interest

Free zones in Nicaragua offer significant tax benefits. Companies operating in free zones may be publicly or privately owned, and must focus their business on the creation and exportation of products. Such companies are exempt from all taxes, including municipal taxes.

As with so many Latin American countries, income from outside of the country is generally exempt, provided that the business or work to earn it was not done in Nicaragua.

Should you be interested in finding out more information about Nicaragua, contact:

The Embassy of Nicaragua
1627 New Hampshire Ave., NW
Washington, DC 20009
Tel: 202-939-6570

The U.S. Mission in Nicaragua
Kilometer 4.5 Carretera Sur.
Managua
Nicaragua
Mailing Address: APO AA 34021
Tel: 505-2-666010, 666013, 666015
Fax: 505-2-669074

Panama

Panama is a republic in Central America, located between Costa Rica and Colombia. To its east lies the Caribbean Sea, while to the west is the Pacific Ocean. The country, which is situated in the isthmus that links North America and South America, is bisected by the Panama Canal. Panama is a long, narrow country with an area of 29,762 square miles (77,082 square kilometers), making it slightly smaller than South Carolina. Rugged mountains, occasionally broken by upland plains, run through the country's interior. Coastal areas are mostly rolling hills and plains.

The climate of Panama is tropical, featuring heat and humidity. The rainy season stretches from May to January, with a drier season from January to May. Annual rainfall on the east coast averages about 117 inches (297 centimeters), and on the west coast 65 inches (165 centimeters). Average annual temperatures in coastal areas range from 73 to 81 degrees F (23 to 27 degrees C). In the higher, interior regions, temperatures are a little cooler, averaging about 66 degrees F (19 degrees C).

Panama has a population of close to 2,655,000 people. Mestizos make up about 70% of Panamanians, West Indians about 14%, whites about 10%, and Indians about 6%. About 85% of Panamanians are Roman Catholics with the remaining 15% belonging to Protestant sects. Spanish is the country's official language, but English is spoken rather widely. Many Panamanians are bilingual, and the literacy rate is 90%.

The standard of living in Panama tends to be better, on average, than that of many Latin American countries. One of the reasons for this has been the long American presence associated with the Panama Canal. With the building of the Canal, Americans also built the infrastructure that was necessary to

143

Residence Havens

support it, including roads, bridges, schools, and hospitals. The Canal was unquestionably the engineering and construction marvel of its age, and continues to be a remarkably efficient enterprise. Health care in Panama is good, reflected in life expectancy rates of 71 years for men and 76 years for women.

Panama offers various recreational activities. Fine restaurants, nightclubs, snorkeling, swimming, surfing, fishing, sailing, mountain climbing, and simple relaxation in a picturesque environment are just some of the ways to pass time in an enjoyable manner. Panama City, the capital, is a modern, bustling commercial center mixing colonial grandeur with modern sophistication. There is plenty to visit in Panama, from the Canal to museums to mountains and beaches.

History and Government

Before the arrival of the Spanish, Panama was inhabited by tribes of Indians including the Cuna, Choco, and Guaymi. Their numbers were quickly overcome through Spanish weaponry and the diseases that accompanied the Spanish from the Old World. The first Spanish settlement was established in Panama at Nombre de Dios in 1510. During the colonial period, Panama's importance to Spain centered on its being the major route of virtually all traffic between Peru and Spain and other Spanish colonies. This route attracted pirates and in time became so dangerous that Spain began using the route around Cape Horn.

In 1821 Panama declared itself free from Spanish rule, and voluntarily became a part of Colombia. This union was not stable, however — mostly because of Panamanian discontent with Colombian rule — and Panama broke away from Colombia in 1840. In 1842, Colombia reestablished its authority over the isthmus, but relations were uneasy and Panamanians longed for full independence. In subsequent years violence erupted frequently.

Panama

In 1846, Colombia signed a treaty with the U.S., permitting Americans to build a railroad across Panama. At this time, Panama was used as a land bridge by Americans journeying from California and Oregon to the East Coast.

The idea of a canal through Panama had been first aired in the 16th century, but the engineering skill and technology to build it were not available. Obtaining permission from the Colombian government, the French tried to build a canal in 1880, but failed, suffering 22,000 deaths from malaria and yellow fever. Intrigued by the possibility of a water route through Central America, the U.S. was willing to take over the building of the canal from the French — who were eager to sell their concession — but Colombia, which was at the time involved in a civil war, refused to sign a treaty giving the U.S. the right to assume control of the canal project.

The interests of the U.S. thus coincided with Panama. When a revolutionary junta declared Panama independent of Colombia, the U.S. immediately recognized the new country, and a treaty between Panama and the U.S., giving the U.S. the right to build the Canal, was soon signed. Of course, the U.S. guaranteed Panamanian independence. A provision of the treaty granting the U.S. foreign rights in perpetuity over the Canal Zone, as well as the right to intervene in Panama's internal affairs, led to much friction between the two countries in upcoming years. Indeed, the U.S. has intervened militarily in Panama often, the most recent time being in 1989 when U.S. forces invaded Panama and ousted Manuel Noriega, a self-appointed president who ran Panama with dictatorial powers.

Although democratic rule was restored after Noriega, Panama's relations with the U.S. continue to be somewhat strained. In recent years the U.S. has resolved to return the Canal to the sovereignty of Panama, an act that will likely improve the relations between the two countries.

Panama is a republic. The chief of state and head of government is the president, who is elected for a five-year term by popular vote. Suffrage,

Residence Havens

which is 18 years of age, is universal and compulsory. The legislative branch of the government is the Legislative Assembly, and the judicial branch includes the Supreme Court, superior courts, and courts of appeal. Panama's laws are based on a system of civil laws.

The Economy of Panama

Panama enjoys a prime location as a link between the Atlantic and Pacific. Its economy is based on commerce, banking, and tourism. Inflation has remained relatively low in recent years, and growth has been steady if somewhat unspectacular. GDP per capita is slightly over $5,000. Panama has an unemployment rate of about 13%, but this is mostly unskilled labor. There is a shortage of skilled labor in Panama.

Panama's infrastructure is sound. Its telecommunications systems are well developed, the country has four major seaports, and air travel connects Panama to all Central American countries as well as North and South America. Miami is the principal departure site from the U.S. to Panama.

Panama's financial system is also highly developed. The country has been evolving into a financial and commercial center, with its banking activities assuming international stature. The balboa is the nation's currency.

Tax Facts of Interest

Although the tax rates on local income are high in Panama, there is no tax on foreign-source income.

In addition, major tax incentives are available for tourism projects. The incentives apply to all areas of tourism, for example, investments in hotels, motels, inns, restaurants, night clubs, recreational enterprises, specialty shops, tourist agencies, and tourist transportation. (Note, these are just some examples; virtually any business that focuses on tourism is eligible.) Tax incentives are substantial, including:

- Up to a 20 years' exemption on real estate taxes.
- Exemption from taxes on assets or capital.
- Exemption from income tax on interest earned by creditors in business operations for investing in hotels.
- If the project is located in one of nine geographical zones set aside for tourist development, a exemption of 15 years from income tax is available.
- For individuals and companies who invest in stocks or bonds issued by tourist companies, a 50% reduction from taxable income is available.

There are several categories of special retirement visas readily available for people who will not be working in Panama.

Should you wish to find out more information about Panama as a possible retirement site, contact:

The Embassy of Panama
2862 McGill Terrace, NW
Washington, DC 20008
Tel: 202-483-1407

Residence Havens

The U.S. Embassy in Panama
Avenida Balboa and Calle 38
Apartado 6959
Panama City 5
Panama

Mailing Address: American Embassy Panama
Unit 0945, APO AA 34002
Tel: 507-227-1377
Fax: 507-227-1964

The Panama Tourist Bureau
P.O. Box 4421
Zone 5
The Republic of Panama
Tel: +507-226-7000 or +507-226-3544
Fax: +507-226-3483 or +507-226-6856

Paraguay

Paraguay is a central, inland republic in South America, surrounded by Bolivia on the northwest and north, Brazil on the east, and Argentina on the south and southwest. Slightly smaller than California, Paraguay has an area of 157,048 square miles (406,752 square kilometers).

A land of physical contrast, Paraguay may be divided into distinct regions: west of Rio Paraguay is the Gran Chaco, a low flat plain; east of Rio Paraguay are grassy plains and wooded hills; and much of the rest of the country is forest and thorny scrub. Paraguay proper, often referred to as the Oriental, consists mainly of the Parana Plateau with an elevation that varies from 1,000 to 2,000 feet (305 to 610 meters).

The climate of Paraguay is subtropical, semiarid in the far west and rather rainy in the east. The forests in the east may receive 60 inches (152 centimeters) of rain annually, while areas in the west (the Gran Chaco) may receive little more than 32 inches (about 80 centimeters). At Asuncion, the capital, rainfall averages about 44 inches (112 centimeters) yearly. Annual average temperatures likewise vary. At Asuncion, the average temperature in July (winter) is about 63 degrees F (17 degrees C); in January (summer), it is about 80 degrees F (26 degrees C). Temperatures in the Gran Chaco and other regions in the north may reach 100 degrees F (37.8 degrees C) in the summer.

Paraguay has a population of some 5,504,000 people. Of these, 95% are Mestizo with the remainder being made up of whites and Amerindians. About 90% of the population is Roman Catholic, with the rest belonging mostly to Protestant denominations. Spanish is the official language of the country, but Guarani is also widely spoken. The literacy rate in Paraguay is about 92%.

Residence Havens

While the standard of living in the major cities is good, quality of life declines as one moves out to remote areas. This is also true of adequate health care, which is not available in all parts of the country. Life expectancy rates are good, however, about 72 years for men and 75 years for women.

In the past, well into the 20th century, Paraguay was a rather rigid society, tightly controlled by its government. It didn't always welcome visitors. More recently however, the country has taken steps to encourage tourists. Life is pleasant and relaxed in Asuncion, which boasts fine restaurants, parks, and theaters. Outside the capital, activities such as hiking, sightseeing, and fishing are enjoyed by many. For some retirees, the quiet, slow pace of life in Paraguay may be a prime consideration.

History and Government

Prior to the Spanish conquest, Paraguay was inhabited by the Guarani and several other hunter-gatherer Indian groups. In 1525 the Portuguese explorer, Alejo Garcia discovered the land that was to become Paraguay, but it was not until 1537 that the Spanish established the first permanent settlement. Unlike other colonies, Paraguay never was tightly controlled by Spain, whose interests were focused elsewhere on the continent. In fact, the crown permitted Jesuit missionaries much local control, and the Jesuits for a time were the strongest power in the colony. Coming to recognize the power of the Jesuits as a threat, the crown expelled the order from Paraguay (as well as the rest of Spanish America) in 1767. In 1776, Spain created the viceroyalty of La Plata, which included the modern countries of Argentina, Uruguay, Bolivia, and Paraguay. Once more, Paraguay slipped into relative unimportance. In 1811, while the rest of Latin America struggled against Spanish authority, Paraguay declared its own independence, an act that went unopposed by Spain.

With independence came difficult times. Dictators, wars, destruction and reconstruction became all too common and lasted well into the 20th century. In the 1990s, Paraguay's political situation has improved significantly. Censorship has been eliminated, opposition parties have been legalized, and basic rights have been supported.

Paraguay is a republic in which the president is the chief of state and head of the government. He is elected for a five-year term via a system of universal and compulsory suffrage of citizens 18 to 60 years of age. The legislature is comprised of the Chamber of Senators and the Chamber of Deputies. Paraguay's legal system is based on old Roman law, and Argentine and French codes. While citizens of Paraguay don't enjoy the same degree of freedom as citizens of some other republics, the country has clearly taken long strides to becoming more democratic and respectful of individual rights.

The Economy of Paraguay

Although Paraguay's economy has grown steadily, if not robustly, in recent years, nearly half of the population works in agriculture. Many farmers are subsistence farmers. Much of the rest of the economy is involved in services, although the government is trying to encourage the growth of light manufacturing and the production of small consumer items, particularly for export. In an attempt to spur economic growth, the government has also attempted reforms which include privatization. GDP per capita, unfortunately, remains low at about $3,200. The unemployment rate is high, mired at about 12%.

Paraguay's infrastructure is weak compared to modern standards. Its telephone system is poor, with reliable service sometimes being hard to obtain even in the capital. Its sea- and airports would benefit greatly from modernization, while only about 5% of its highways are paved.

Since 1995, when the government was forced to intercede in a bank crisis, attempts have been made to strengthen the financial system. Although banks in the major cities offer various services to consumers and businesses, their long-term stability and strength should be regarded with caution. The country's currency is the guarani.

Tax Facts of Interest

Like most Latin American countries, Paraguay has a variety of taxes. However, <u>foreign-source income is exempt</u>. For the retiree who wishes to reside in a land that remains relatively isolated from the rest of the world, that tax benefit might prove to be most advantageous.

Should you wish to find out more information about Paraguay, contact:

The Embassy of Paraguay
2400 Massachusetts Ave., NW
Washington, DC 20008
Tel: 202-483-6960
Fax: 202-234-4508

The U.S. Embassy in Paraguay
1776 Avenida Mariscal Lopez
Casilla Postal 402
Asuncion
Paraguay
Mailing Address: Unit 4711
 APO AA 34036-0001
Tel: 595-21-213-715
Fax: 595-21-213-728

Philippines

The Republic of the Philippines is located in southeastern Asia, between the Philippine Sea and South China Sea. It is an archipelago, about 750 miles (1,210 kilometers) east of Vietnam. The country is composed of about 7,100 islands, of which only about 450 are more than one square mile (2.6 square kilometers) in area. Eleven islands have an area of more than 1,000 square miles (about 2,600 square kilometers). These islands — Luzon, Mindanao, Samar, Negros, Palawan, Panay, Mindoro, Leyte, Cebu, Bohol, and Masbate — are home to most of the country's 75,000,000 people. The total land area of the Philippines is about 115,830 square miles (about 300,000 square kilometers), slightly larger than Arizona.

The topography of the islands that comprise the Philippines is mostly mountains bordered by coastal lowlands. The islands are of volcanic origin, and the region remains seismically active. Earthquakes are not uncommon, and about 20 active volcanoes are found on the islands. The larger islands, particularly Luzon and Mindanao, possess broad plains and fertile valleys as well as mountains. Apo Volcano is on Mindanao, and at 9,692 feet (2,954 meters) is the highest point in the Philippines.

The climate of the Philippines is tropical marine with a northeast monsoon from November to April and a southwest monsoon from May to October. The mean annual temperature across the islands is about 80 degrees F (27 degrees C). This translates to average maximum summer temperatures of 92 to 94 degrees F (33 to 34 degrees C) and average winter temperatures of 84 to 88 degrees F (29 to 31 degrees C). Rainfall throughout the islands is rather heavy, with about 80 inches (about 200 centimeters) falling in the lowlands

153

annually. The wet season typically runs from June to October with heavy rains and the threat of typhoons (the Pacific equivalent of Atlantic hurricanes).

Of the Philippines' population of 75,000,000, Christian Malays comprise about 91%, Muslim Malays 4%, Chinese 1.5%, with the rest being made up of various minority groups. About 83% of the country's residents are Roman Catholic, with 9% being Protestant, 5% Muslim, and Buddhist and other groups making up the remainder. The country has two official languages: Pilipino, which is based on Tagalog, and English, which is spoken throughout the country and is the language of business and government. Numerous local dialects are spoken throughout the islands. The country's literacy rate is about 95%.

Like many of the countries of the Pacific, the Philippines has undertaken an impressive modernization program. One of the results of this program has been the improvement in the quality of life. This is especially true in the major cities where the standard of living and health care are considered to be quite good. Like most developing countries, however, this quality of life does not extend to every part of the nation. As one moves farther from the cities, health care and living standards decline. This is reflected in the nation's life expectancy rates of 63 years for men and 68 years for women.

The Philippines is a country where numerous cultures have come together. While the great majority of its people are Indonesian and Malaysian, Chinese, Spanish, and American influence is pronounced. Indeed, American influence, particularly its language, has resulted in the Philippines becoming the third-largest English speaking nation in the world.

The islands are known for their rich variety of entertainment and activities. With some of the most renowned coral reefs in the world, the Philippines are a noted site for scuba diving. Other attractions include fishing, swimming, and golf. Malls, supermarkets, and fashion boutiques carry items to fit just about everyone's needs, tastes, and budget. Dining at world-class restaurants is also a favorite pastime of many, as is taking part in the exciting nightlife that

Manila offers. Music played in clubs varies from rock and roll and Broadway hits to traditional Filipino music and dance.

Housing is also attractive in the Philippines. Quality homes, hotels, and recreational facilities are found in and around the country's majors cities. Moreover, an excellent standard of living can be obtained for a low cost. The Philippines are, without question, a retirement haven of considerable attraction.

History and Government

The Philippines are thought to have been inhabited for roughly 250,000 years. The islands' first inhabitants most likely came from China and the Malayan Archipelago. Successive migrations brought new people from southeast Asia, Vietnam, Indonesia, and the Malay Peninsula. As early as the third century B.C., island dwellers carried on trade with Arabia, India, and China. In time, the Chinese gained nominal control of the islands and placed governors there to ensure Chinese interests.

The first European to visit the Philippines was the Spanish explorer Ferdinand Magellan, who discovered the islands during his voyage to circumnavigate the world, but it was not until 1542 that the Spanish named the archipelago the Islas Filipinas, or Philippine Islands, in honor of their king, Philip II. In 1564 the Spanish were able to establish a permanent settlement. During the colonial period, the Portuguese, English, and Dutch all attempted to seize control of the islands from Spain, however, the attempts were unsuccessful and the islands remained under Spanish control until 1898. This was the year the U.S. defeated Spain in the Spanish-American War and was given control of the Philippines. During World War II, the islands were occupied by the Japanese, and the U.S. did not fully regain control until the Japanese officially surrendered in September of 1945. The Philippines gained their independence from the U.S. in 1946.

The Philippines is a republic, with its capital at Manila. The head of the government and chief of state is the president, who is elected for a six-year term by popular vote. The legislative branch of the government is comprised of a bicameral congress, the Senate and House of Representatives. The country's judiciary is founded on Spanish and Angle-American law. Most Americans will find that the government of the Philippines is based quite closely on the federal system of the U.S. This is another of America's lasting influences.

The Economy of the Philippines

The Philippine economy is mostly based on agriculture and light industry. Some of the country's most notable agricultural products include: rice, coconuts, corn, bananas, pineapples, sugarcane, mangoes, and fish. Major industries include: textiles, chemicals, wood products, food processing, electronics assembly, petroleum refining, fishing, pharmaceuticals, and fishing. Per capita GDP is about U.S.$2,500.

While the infrastructure throughout the islands, overall, is adequate, it is best in the major cities. The telephone system is reliable domestically, while overseas services are good. Numerous airports are found throughout the islands, with international airports in Manila and Cebu. Major airlines from around the world have regularly scheduled flights to the Philippines. The islands also have several seaports equipped to handle modern vessels.

The country's financial system is good. Banks provide a variety of services and major credit cards and travelers checks are widely accepted. The peso is the unit of currency. Most foreign currencies can easily be exchanged for pesos at banks, hotels, and authorized foreign exchange dealers.

The government has taken steps in recent years to support industrial development, primarily through programs of incentives, improvement of infrastructure, and a restructuring of the tax system. This is where potential tax advantages may be found by individuals considering retirement in the Philippines.

Tax Facts of Interest

While all individuals are required to pay income tax, <u>there is no local income tax and inheritance tax in the Philippines. Exemptions from tax include royalties, interest from Philippine bank deposits, dividends from local corporations, and capital gains from sales of shares of stocks.</u> However, numerous tax advantages and incentives are available to investors. Thus, an individual who is considering retirement in the near future might find investment in the Philippines to be beneficial. These benefits can be summed up as follows.

The Omnibus Investment Code provides a set of benefits to local and foreign investors in high-priority economic activities, including:

- An income tax holiday.
- Importation of capital equipment and spare parts, tax and duty-free.
- An additional deduction of labor expenses from taxable income.
- A tax credit on capital equipment that is obtained from local sources.
- An exemption from national or local contractors' tax.
- Simplified customs procedures.
- Employment of foreign nationals.

If a company locates facilities in an area that the government has classified as a less-developed area, additional incentives are possible, including:

- A complete deduction from taxable income of costs necessary for infrastructure and public facilities in the area.
- A double-deduction of labor expenses.

If a company locates facilities in an export processing zone, it will be eligible for the following:

- An exemption from local taxes, licenses, and fees.
- A special tax on merchandise within the zone.
- An exemption from real estate taxes regarding production equipment not attached to the land.
- An exemption from the 15% branch profits remittance tax.
- An exemption from SGS inspection.

The government of the Philippines strongly encourages investment, and has drafted legislation to make the Philippines a business-friendly country. This outlook clearly provides investors with significant benefits, making the Philippines a potentially excellent retirement haven.

Should you wish to find out more information about the Philippines, contact:

The Philippine Department of Tourism
556 Fifth Ave.
New York, NY 10036
Tel: 212-575-7915

The Embassy of the Philippines
1600 Massachusetts Ave., NW
Washington, DC 20036
Tel: 202-467-9300

Fax: 202-328-7614

U.S. Embassy in the Philippines
1201 Roxas Boulevard
Ermita, Manila 1000
Mailing Address: APO AP 96440
Tel: 63-2-521-71-16
Fax: 63-2-522-43-61

Philippine Department of Tourism
T.M. Kalaw Street
Rizal Park
Metro Manila
Philippines
P.O. Box 3451
Tel: 02-599031

Philippine Department of Tourism
199 Piccadilly
London W1V 9LE
United Kingdom
Tel: 071-439-3481

Philippine Department of Tourism
Kaiserstrasse 15
6000 Frankfurt am Main 1
Frankfurt
Germany
Tel: 069-893-9495

Philippine Department of Tourism
21/F, Regent Centre
88 Queen's Road, Central HK
Hong Kong
Tel: 05-267592

*Philippine Department of Tourism
2/F, Dainan Bldg.
2-19-23 Shinmachi
Nishi-ku, Osaka 550
Japan
Tel: 06-5355-07172*

St. Kitts and Nevis

St. Kitts and Nevis are islands in the Caribbean Sea located about one-third of the way from Puerto Rico to Trinidad and Tobago. The islands, which are volcanic and mountainous, have a total area of about 102 square miles (about 269 square kilometers). The highest point is Mount Liamuiga, about 3,700 feet (1,156 meters).

The islands enjoy a subtropical climate. There is little seasonal variation in temperature, however, a rainy season occurs between May and November. The average annual temperature is about 80 degrees F (27 degrees C). Rainfall varies, from about 50-80 inches (125-200 centimeters) annually. The driest part of the year is from January to April, and the wettest part is from May to November.

About 41,000 people live on St. Kitts and Nevis. The majority of the islands' inhabitants are descended from Africans, and the major religions on the islands are various Protestant sects and Roman Catholicism. The language most widely spoken is English, and the literacy rate is 97%. Health care is good and the standard of living attainable is excellent.

Indeed, the islands have evolved into a tropical paradise where natural beauty gives rise to a host of recreational activities such as golf, tennis, water skiing, windsurfing, snorkeling, scuba diving, boating, bicycling, horseback riding, hiking, mountain climbing, fishing, and swimming. Of course, fine dining and leisurely shopping are also important pastimes. Several duty-free shops are on the islands, selling a variety of products and items. Despite all of these recreations, the islands have managed to maintain a quiet, less frenetic pace of life than many of the other Caribbean islands.

Residence Havens

Tranquil and *relaxed* are often used to describe the pace of life on St. Kitts and Nevis, which, for many, can be a marvelous retirement haven.

History and Government

St. Kitts was originally inhabited by the Native American tribe of the Caribs, who likely came to the island in the 13th century. Christopher Columbus discovered St. Kitts in 1493, and he named the island for his patron saint, St. Christopher. Columbus then discovered Nevis, the island to the south, naming it Nuestra Senora de las Nieves, "Our Lady of the Snows," because on the day he saw it the island's cloud-covered features reminded him of the snows of the Pyrenees. From that early name, the island has come to be called Nevis.

Although the Spanish maintained claims to the island, in 1623 the island became the site of the first successful English settlement in the West Indies. During the 17th and 18th centuries, the French seized the islands several times, but finally returned control to England in accordance with the Treaty of Paris, 1783. In 1871, St. Kitts, Nevis, and Anguilla were united as a British dependency. In 1967 St. Kitts and Nevis became members of the West Indies Associated States, then, in 1983, the two islands formed a federation with their capital at Basseterre.

Because of their close ties to Great Britain, the chief of state is the queen, who is represented by the governor general. The head of the government is the prime minister who is appointed by the governor general. The islands' legislature is the House of Assembly, and the judicial system is based on English common law. Suffrage is universal for adults.

The Economy of St. Kitts and Nevis

The economy of St. Kitts and Nevis has traditionally depended on agriculture, however, tourism and light manufacturing for export have become increasingly important. The federation's GDP per capita is U.S.$5,400, and the rates of inflation and unemployment are low.

The islands possess a relatively good infrastructure. Telecommunications services are good, the islands have two seaports, at Basseterre and Charlestown, and two airports.

The financial system of the islands is modern and efficient, providing the various services consumers expect. The basic unit of currency is the Eastern Caribbean dollar. U.S. dollars are also considered legal tender on the islands, and major credit cards are widely accepted.

Tax Facts of Interest

There are no personal income taxes in St. Kitts and Nevis.

Should you be interested in finding out more information about St. Kitts and Nevis, contact:

The Embassy of St. Kitts and Nevis
3216 New Mexico Ave., NW
Washington, DC 20016
Tel: 202-686-2636
Fax: 202-686-5740

St. Kitts Tourist Board
Pelican Mall
Basseterre, St. Kitts
St. Kitts and Nevis
Tel: 869-465-2620
Fax: 869-465-8794

Residence Havens

*Nevis Tourist Board
Main St.
Charlestown, Nevis
St. Kitts and Nevis
Tel: +1-869-469-1042
Fax: +1-869-469-1066*

St. Martin (St. Maarten)

St. Martin is one of the Leeward Islands in the West Indies, positioned between the islands of Anguilla and St. Barthelemy. The northern part of the island, often referred to as Saint-Martin, is a dependency of France. The southern part, often called Sint Maarten, is a part of the Netherlands Antilles and is internally self-governing.

St. Martin is the smallest island in the world to be shared by two separate nations. The border between the French and Dutch parts of the island is open and people are free to travel back and forth. A spirit of friendly cooperation has prevailed on the island for about 350 years.

The island is quite small, about 33 square miles (86 square kilometers) in total area, of which 20 square miles (52 square kilometers) is French and 13 square miles (34 square kilometers) is Dutch. While the western coast is relatively low-lying, much of the Dutch part of the island is rather hilly. The coastline is dotted with numerous bays, lagoons, and truly spectacular beaches.

Like the rest of the islands in the Netherlands Antilles, St. Martin enjoys a tropical climate, which is moderated by the northeast trade winds. The island is sunny and warm throughout the year, making it an ideal and popular tourist site. Temperatures average 82 degrees F (about 28 degrees C) in summer, and just a few degrees cooler in the winter. Rainfall averages about 45 inches (about 110 centimeters) per year, with late summer and early fall seeing the most amount of precipitation.

About 28,000 people live in the French part of St. Martin, and close to 32,000 live in the Dutch part. The population has descended from Africans, English, Spanish, Portuguese, Dutch, and French. Major religions are Roman Catholicism, various Protestant sects, and Judaism. While Dutch is the official

165

Residence Havens

language of Dutch St. Martin, and French is the official language of French St. Martin, English is spoken widely. Papiamento, a local dialect of Spanish-Portuguese-Dutch-English, and Spanish are also spoken throughout the islands. The literacy rate approaches 98%. The standard of living and health care of the island are very good.

Although the Dutch and French parts of the island have much in common, they also retain their individuality. Dutch Sint Maarten is the busier and livelier of the two. It has the biggest hotels, and Queen Juliana Airport, and its capital of Philipsburg is bustling and more cosmopolitan than the French capital at Marigot. On the whole, the French portion of the island is a bit quieter and more relaxed. Both parts of the island, however, offer incredibly beautiful beaches, fine restaurants, an exciting nightlife, including gambling, and plenty of island recreations including a variety of watersports, golf, and tennis. Moreover, the entire island is one of the best free ports in the world with no duties or taxes placed on imported or exported goods. On even the most exclusive items, shoppers can save up to a third or more on prices they would typically pay elsewhere. In some cases savings reach 50%. Indeed, shoppers and cruise ships from around the world make St. Martin a destination for the savings available on pricey items. St. Martin is potentially an excellent retirement haven.

History and Government

Christopher Columbus discovered St. Martin in 1493, and by the 1630s both the Dutch and French had established settlements. In 1648 the two sides agreed to divide the island, and since then the inhabitants have lived there in a spirit of neighborly harmony.

According to legend, when the French and Dutch sought a way to divide the island, it was agreed that a Frenchman and Dutchman would meet on the beach at dawn, stand back to back, and begin walking forward. From the point they started to the point they met would be the end points of the border. It has been said that each man took a drink with him to quench his thirst beneath the hot Caribbean sun. The Frenchman took a bottle of wine, and the Dutchman took gin. According to the story (perhaps because gin is more potent than wine), the Dutchman meandered a bit on his way and walked less than the Frenchman. Thus, the French got the bigger portion of the island. Of course, it's more likely that the measurements of those doing the dividing were simply in error.

Technically, the French part of the island is a dependency of the French Department of Guadeloupe, which is 160 miles to the southwest. The Dutch part of the island is part of the Netherlands Antilles, which is a dependency of the Netherlands. Dutch St. Martin enjoys internal self-governing.

The Economy of St. Martin

Tourism is the principal sector of the island's economy. Compared to many other Caribbean islands, St. Martin has a high per capita income and a well-developed infrastructure. Telecommunications, air- and seaports possess modern equipment and are reliable and dependable.

Geared as they are to the tourist trade, both the French and Dutch sides of the island have a modern financial system. Money is easily exchangeable, and major credit cards are accepted.

Tax Facts of Interest

St. Martin is one of the world's best free ports. No taxes or duties are paid on items coming in or going out. This can result in savings of up to 50% on the prices of items bought elsewhere. Items including expensive jewelry, electronics, perfumes, and crystal are some of the most popular.

Residence Havens

Should you be interested in finding out more about St. Martin, contact:

The St. Maarten Tourist Office
675 Third Ave., Suite 1806
New York, NY 10017
Tel: 212-953-2084 or 800 ST. MAARTEN
Fax: 212-953-2145

St. Maarten Tourist Bureau
Walter Nisbeth Rd., 23
Philipsburg, St. Maarten
Netherlands Antilles
Tel: 011-5995-22337
Fax: 011-5995-22734

Office du Tourisme de Saint-Martin
Waterfront, north side of the harbor
Marigot, Saint-Martin
Guadeloupe
Tel: +590-87-57-21
Fax: +590-87-56-43

French West Indies Tourist Board
444 Madison Ave.
New York, NY 10022
Tel: 900-990-0040 (95 cents per minute)

French Government Tourist Office
645 N. Michigan Ave., Suite 3360
Chicago, IL 60611
Tel: 312-751-7800

French Government Tourist Office
1981 Avenue McGill College, Suite 490
Montreal, Quebec H3A 2W9
Canada
Tel: 514-288-4264

St.Martin (St.Maarten)

*French Government Tourist Office
30 St. Patrick Street, Suite 700
Toronto, Ontario M5T 3A3
Canada
Tel: 416-593-6427*

Seychelles

Seychelles consists of some 118 islands in the Indian Ocean, northeast of Madagascar. The total area of the archipelago is about 108 square miles (280 square kilometers).

The country is composed of two relatively distinct island groups: the Mahe group in the north, which contains the country's most important islands, and the coral islands that stretch to the south. The Mahe group is made up of 40 islands, most of which possess hilly interiors, some rising to heights of nearly 3,000 feet (about 900 meters). The major islands of the Mahe group are Mahe Island, which is the largest of the archipelago, Praslin, Silhouette, and La Digue. Most of the coral islands to the south lack adequate water resources and are uninhabited.

Seychelles has a tropical marine climate. Late May to September is the cooler season during the southeast monsoon, while March to May is the warmer season during the northwest monsoon. The average annual temperature is about 75 degrees F (24 degrees C), with seasonal variation of only a few degrees. Rainfall varies among the islands, but averages about 90 inches (233 centimeters) per year.

Some 77,500 people live in Seychelles. Most of the population has descended from Asians, Africans, and Europeans. Close to 90% of the residents are Roman Catholics, about 8% are Anglicans, and the rest profess other religions. English and French are official languages, although Creole — a mix of the many languages once spoken on the islands but based mostly on French — is also widely spoken.

Although Seychelles has made rapid strides in modernization, the standard of living, particularly outside Victoria, the capital, and its surroundings, trail those of more developed lands. The life expectancy rate is 64 years for men and 74 years for women. The literacy rate is only about 58%.

Despite these concerns, Seychelles is fast becoming one of the Eastern Hemisphere's premier tourist sites. While tourism is the mainstay of the economy (about 100,000 people visit Seychelles annually), the government has initiated programs that strongly encourage investment. One of the aims of these initiatives is to make Seychelles an offshore banking and international business center. The policy is paying o ff, as the country has been moving forward aggressively, an important result of which is its improving standard of living.

Seychelles offers large and small hotels, guest houses, and island escapes. Activities include fine dining and entertainment, diving, sailing and fishing in one of the most beautiful and unspoiled natural environments in the world. Within the past few years Seychelles has become a retirement haven worthy of serious consideration.

History and Government

It is thought that as early as the 9th century the Arabs knew of the islands that were to become Seychelles, possibly even having visited them often. Knowledge of the archipelago, however, did not come to Europe until after the Portuguese discovered the islands in 1502. At this time the islands were uninhabited and remained so until 1756 when the French claimed them. In 1770 the French began settlement, but in 1811 the British occupied the islands and gained control. In 1903 the islands were made a separate British dependency, and in 1976 they were granted independence. It is interesting that although the British controlled the islands longer than the French, the islands received their name from Vicomte Moreau de Seychelles, who was the controller-general of finance during the reign of Louis XV of France.

Seychelles is a republic with the capital located at Victoria. The president, who is elected for a five-year term by popular vote, is the chief of state and head of the government. The People's Assembly is the legislative branch of the government, and is responsible for laws that are based on English common law, French civil law, and customary law.

The Economy of Seychelles

In the years since independence, 1976, the economy of Seychelles has been, overall, robust. Per capita output, for example, has increased seven times over the near-subsistence levels which were common earlier. While the government still supports tourism, which continues to be the major part of the islands' economy, it has also embarked upon an impressive program of development focusing on offshore banking, freeport and export processing zones, and the promotion of Seychelles as a financial and business center. The country's per capita GDP is about U.S.$6,000.

The infrastructure on Seychelles is considered to be one of the best of the countries in this region of the world. Telecommunications are dependable and reliable and provide easy access to places throughout the world. The country has an international airport that is able to handle the modern aircraft, and is the backbone to the tourist industry. Port Victoria is the deepest port of the Indian Ocean and is known as one of the most efficient ports in the region.

As one would expect, with Seychelles attempting to develop an offshore banking industry, its banking services are quite modern and efficient. The country's currency is officially the Seychelles rupee.

Residence Havens

Tax Facts of Interest

Seychelles offers numerous tax advantages. Perhaps most importantly, <u>there is no income tax</u>.

In addition, Seychelles is a pure tax haven for companies. The Investment Promotion Act (IPA) was enacted in 1994 to encourage investment in Seychelles. The act addresses businesses that serve both the domestic sector and those whose major activity is exports.

Following are some of the incentives included with the government's general investment policies:

- No personal income tax.
- 100% foreign ownership.
- No withholding tax on dividends.
- 100% repatriation of capital and profits.
- Accelerated depreciation.
- No wealth tax, gift tax, property tax, capital gains tax, death duties, or taxes on properties.
- Reasonable rates on corporate tax, social security, and incidental benefits.

In addition the Investment Promotion Act offers the following features:

- Local and foreign owned businesses are eligible.
- No import duties on capital equipment.
- Accelerated depreciation schedules of up to 150% of original cost of asset for certain categories of investments.

Seychelles

- Low business tax rate of 15% with further tax credits possible, resulting in an effective tax rate of 9%.
- In some instances, businesses may be able to enjoy a tax holiday.

Seychelles has also made trust registration easy and valuable, including the following:

- Transfer or disposition by an individual creating an international trust cannot be made invalid by any foreign rule of forced heirship.
- The accumulation of income is not restricted.
- There is no requirement to mention the names of the settlor and the name of the beneficiary, with the exception that the latter is a Seychellois national or a body corporate resident in the country.
- International trusts are valid and enforceable in Seychelles.
- Laws governing an international trust is the law selected by the settlor to be the proper law; this choice may be express or implied in the terms of the trust.
- Confidentiality is maintained. Moreover it is prohibited to disclose or produce information or documents relating to an international trust. The only exception to this is an injunction of the Seychelles Supreme Court.
- A registration fee of U.S.$100.

Under the International Trade Zone Act, which allows for the licensing of both freeport operations and manufacturing, <u>companies that are eligible for an ITZ license are exempt from all taxes</u>, as long as their output is geared towards an export market.

Residence Havens

Without question Seychelles is positioning itself as a business and financial center which will have far-reaching effects on its residents. Should you be interested in finding out more information about Seychelles, contact:

>*Seychelles Department of Tourism and Transport*
>*Independence House, Victoria*
>*P.O. Box 92*
>*Mahe*
>*Seychelles*
>*Tel: 248-225313, 224030*
>*Fax: 248-224035, 225131*

>*Embassy of Seychelles*
>*820 Second Ave., Suite 900 F*
>*New York, NY 10017*
>*Tel: 212-687-9766, 9767*
>*Fax: 212-922-9177*

>*U.S. Embassy in Seychelles*
>*4th Floor, Victoria House*
>*Box 251*
>*Victoria, Mahe*
>*Mailing Address: Box 148, Victoria*
>*Unit 62501*
>*APO AE 09815-2501*
>*Tel: 248-225256*
>*Fax: 248-225189*

Tunisia

Tunisia is in North Africa, between Algeria and Libya and bordering the Mediterranean Sea. Slightly larger than Georgia, Tunisia has an area of 63,170 square miles (163,610 square kilometers). In the north, Tunisia is mostly mountainous. The mountains give way to a central plain, which in turn eventually merges with the Sahara.

The climate of Tunisia is closely related to its topography. In the north the climate is temperate with mild, rainy winters and hot, dry summers. As one moves farther south, conditions become dryer and desertlike. In the north, temperatures average 79 degrees F (about 26 degrees C) in the summer, and 51 degrees F (about 11 degrees C) in the winter. Rainfall in the north averages about 24 inches (61 centimeters) per year, while in the south precipitation may be less than 7 inches (about 17 centimeters) annually. Overall, the country is dry.

Tunisia has about 9,000,000 people. The great majority of the country's people are Arab-Berber, about 98%, with Europeans comprising about 1% and Jews and others the remaining 1%. Religion follows ethnic lines: 98% Muslim, 1% Christian, and 1% Jewish. The literacy rate of Tunisia is about 67%.

The standard of living in Tunis, the capital, is good. Health care is of high quality and residents are able to enjoy the typical conveniences people in advanced countries take for granted. An indication of the country's system of health care is its life expectancy rates: 71 years for men and 74 years for women. A variety of recreational pursuits are available, including golf, tennis, hunting, riding, surfing, sailing, and hiking. Fine restaurants, clubs, and shopping are enjoyed by many. On the whole, one can enjoy a pleasant lifestyle, which,

177

along with tax incentives — aimed particularly at businesses — qualifies Tunisia as a potential retirement haven.

History and Government

Tunisia first appears in history books as a part of the Carthaginian Empire. It is generally accepted that Phoenician traders founded the city of Carthage near the site of present-day Tunis in about 814 B.C. For a time, Carthage dominated northern Africa and much of the Mediterranean. That dominance ended with Rome, which, after a series of wars, defeated Carthage and destroyed the city in 146 B.C. For nearly the next 600 years, Tunisia was part of the Roman Empire. In the 5th century A.D. the Vandals, a Germanic tribe, moved southward through the Iberian Peninsula, crossed the Mediterranean, and seized Tunisia, ruling it for roughly a hundred years.

In the following centuries, Tunisia was occupied and controlled by Arabs, Spanish, and Turks, each group leaving behind some influence. In 1881 the French entered Tunisia from Algeria in an operation whose purpose was to curb the activities of Arab tribesman. Tunisia wound up becoming a French protectorate. French influence on Tunisia was profound. French settlers, businessman, and administrators arrived, the result being the introduction of western ideals and practices to the country. The French maintained control until 1956, when in response to Tunisian demands, gave the country its independence. In 1957, Tunisia established itself as a republic.

Tunisia's government is based on a constitution first adopted in 1959, and amended in 1988. Laws are founded on the French civil law system and Islamic law. The chief of state is the president, who is elected for a five-year term by universal suffrage, and the head of government is the prime minister, who is appointed by the president. The legislative branch of government is the Chamber of Deputies. Suffrage is 20 years of age and universal.

The Economy of Tunisia

Tunisia has built a diverse economy, its most important sectors being agriculture, energy, mining, tourism, and manufacturing. In recent years, in an effort to expand the economy, the government has undertaken a program of increasing privatization and tax simplification. Throughout much of the nineties, the growth rate has averaged between 4% and 5%. GDP per capita is U.S.$4,250.

Tunisia's infrastructure, in many respects, surpasses that of most African nations in quality and reliability. The telecommunications system, for example, is adequate both domestically and internationally. The country has several seaports and airports.

In its attempt to attract business and investment, Tunisia has developed a financial system that is flexible and efficient in meeting the needs of businesses and consumers. Overall, the country's banks are considered to be sound, a result of the government imposing strict requirements to strengthen and stabilize the country's financial system.

Tunisia's currency is the dinar. While it is commercially convertible for trade and investment operations, the dinar is still subject to some restrictions, most notably that it is illegal to take Tunisian bank notes and coins in or out of the country. However, there is no limit to the amount of foreign currency visitors can bring into Tunisia and exchange for dinars. It should be noted that nonresidents are exempt from most exchange regulations.

Residence Havens

Tax Facts of Interest

Tunisia offers substantial tax benefits in regard to free trade zones. It should be noted that foreign firms enjoy the same investment incentives as Tunisian companies. <u>Companies operating in free zones are exempt from taxes and customs duties, except social security taxes for employees who choose to participate in the Tunisian social security system.</u> In addition, the following benefits are offered:

- <u>Employees with nonresident status pay a flat income</u> tax rate of 20%, and are exempt from customs duties and taxes on imports of personal goods, including one <u>car per employee.</u>

- <u>Nonresident companies located in a free zone that have</u> a commercial relationship with other companies outside Tunisia, or with companies located within the free <u>zone, are not subject to control. Furthermore,</u> payments made within the free zone may be made either in foreign currency or in convertible dinars. The companies are also guaranteed the transfer of foreign currency capital invested in a free zone and the <u>income derived from it.</u>

Should you be interested in finding out more information about Tunisia, contact:

> *The Embassy of Tunisia*
> *1515 Massachusetts Ave., NW*
> *Washington, DC 20005*
> *Tel: 202-862-1850*

> *U.S. Embassy in Tunisia*
> *144 Avenue de la Liberte*
> *1002 Tunis-Belvedere*
> *Tunisia*
> *Tel: 216-1-782-566*
> *Fax: 216-1-789-719*

Turkey

Turkey has often been considered to be a bridge between Europe and Asia. Located partly in southeastern Europe and partly in southwestern Asia, its position makes it a crossroads between east and west. Bulgaria and Greece border Turkey on the northwest, Georgia, Armenia, and the Black Sea lie to the west, Iran is to the east, to the south lie Iraq, Syria, and the Mediterranean Sea, while to the west waits the Aegean Sea.

Being about 300,000 square miles (780,500 square kilometers), Turkey is a big country, about the twice the size of California. Its topography includes fertile plains and excellent farm land, hills, plateaus, mountains and valleys. At 16,946 feet (5,165 meters), Mount Ararat, recorded in the Bible as the site on which Noah's Ark landed, is the highest peak in the country.

Turkey's climate varies, due to its great area and elevations. Near the shores of the Aegean and Mediterranean seas the climate is highlighted by rainy winters and long, hot summers. Winters are cold and summers are hot in the central part of the country. While the eastern highlands are known for their severe winters, the southeastern part of the country experiences the hottest summers with temperatures averaging more than 86 degrees F (30 degrees C). Rainfall also varies. Precipitation is most abundant along the shores of the Aegean and Mediterranean, decreasing gradually as one moves to the interior.

Turkey has a population of about 62,000,000. About 80% of its people are Turks, with about 20% being Kurds. Many languages are spoken in the country, but by far the most common is Turkish, which up to 90% of the residents speak. Close to 10% of the population speak Kurdish and Arabic. About 99% of Turkey's people are Muslim, most being Sunnite Muslim. Shiites, however, are a significant minority and are most populous in the

Residence Havens

southeastern portions of the country. Christians and other religious groups constitute the final 1%.

In the past two decades Turkey has undertaken impressive steps to improve the quality of life and raise the standard of living for its people. As recent as the early 1980s, for example, nearly four out of every ten Turks was illiterate; the literacy rate today is close to 80% and continues to increase. Health care, too, has shown marked improvement. For men the life expectancy rate is 69 years, while for women it is 73. Health care is considered good in the major cities and towns, but declines in quality as one moves to isolated or remote areas.

Turkey is a captivating land with a fascinating history. Its culture is an exotic blending of east and west, unique in the world. In the major cities and their suburbs, life in turkey includes all of the modern pleasures that may be found in any modern country. With a host of special tax benefits, particularly aimed at business and industry, Turkey is an important addition to the retirement list.

History and Government

Turkey has an ancient history. Civilizations including the Hittites, Phrygians, Lydians, Greeks, and Romans all left their mark on Turkey. After the fall of the Roman Empire in the West, the legacy of Rome, centered in Constantinople and the Byzantine Empire, continued for the next thousand years. In 1453 the great city of Constantinople finally fell to the Ottoman Turks, who ruled their own vast empire for the next four centuries. After World War I Turkey suffered much internal conflict, which led to the Turkish War for Independence. A republic was formed in 1923.

The government of modern Turkey is based on a constitution of 1982. The head of government is the prime minister, who represents the majority party in parliament. The chief of state is the president, who is chosen by parliament for a seven-year term. Legislative power resides with the Grand National Assembly.

Turkey has had a stormy history since its independence, with democratic forces struggling with the military for control of the country. Civilian authority came to power in 1983 and the country has remained under civilian authority since then.

The Economy of Turkey

In the past agriculture was the principal part of Turkey's economy. During the past two decades, however, the government has initiated programs aimed at supporting and expanding the industrial sector. By the early 1990s, industrial production surpassed agriculture in share of the economy. Throughout much of the nineties, Turkey's economy has been expanding rapidly, at some points averaging between 5% and 6%. Clearly, Turkey is benefiting from the increased economic activity throughout eastern Europe and the Balkans, which is expected to continue. Turkish firms are also expanding into Central Asia, which represents a potentially enormous market. Without question, because of its prime location, its culture, language, and the business spirit of the country, Turkey should continue to profit handsomely from its contacts and relations with its neighbors.

Turkey's infrastructure is most developed in and around its major cities such as Ankara, the capital, Istanbul, and Izmir. Such places are linked with quality telecommunications and roads. Important air- and seaports also enjoy solid infrastructure. In remote regions, however, infrastructure is not equal to that of advanced nations. Aware that future economic growth depends upon the quality of the country's infrastructure, the government has embarked on a program of infrastructure modernization.

Residence Havens

Turkey's financial system is generally sound, and is responsive to both the needs of businesses and consumers. The banking system offers the same services provided by banks in nations with advanced economies. The country's currency, the Lira, is almost completely convertible.

Tax Facts of Interest

Although Turkey does not offer many tax exemptions to individuals, the following is noteworthy — nonresidents who live six months or less during the calendar year are required to pay income tax only on income accrued in Turkey.

Turkey does provide important tax benefits in regards to investors. Establishment of a business in a free zone, for example, may bestow numerous advantages, including:

- An exemption for corporate taxes. Rates of an investment allowance may be between 20% and 70% of the total fixed investment, depending on the location of the investment.
- An exemption from taxes for building and construction.
- An exemption from customs duties. Machinery and equipment that are imported are exempt from customs duties, fees, and taxes, the exception being for a fund payment that varies between 5% and 20%.
- In Priority Development Regions, an energy incentive is available.
- On machinery and equipment that is imported, a VAT deferral is possible.
- On machinery and equipment that is procured locally, a VAT refund is possible.
- A deferral for expenditures for research and development.

For business involved in export activities, the following additional incentives are available:

- Exemptions for taxes, duties, and charges.
- An exemption from VAT.
- Incentives for energy use.
- Customs duties exemptions regarding raw materials imported for export products.
- Credits through the Export/Import Bank for exports.
- Credits for pre-shipment export.
- Credits for revolving exports.

Turkey currently has five free zones in operation; six additional sites are under construction. A variety of business activity is permitted in the free zones, including manufacturing, packing, trading, banking, and storage. Companies operating from the free zones enjoy a 100% exemption from all taxes.

For the investor who wishes to establish a business in a suitable country, his or her eventual goal being retirement, Turkey offers many options. Should you like to find out more information about Turkey, contact:

American Turkish Council
1010 Vermont Ave., NW, Suite 1020
Washington, DC 20005-4902
Tel: 202-783-0483
Fax: 202-783-0511

General Directorate of Foreign Investment
Inonu Bulvan 06510 Emek
Ankara, Turkey
Tel: 90-312-212-8914-5
Fax: 90-312-212-8916

Turkey Desk
Department of Trade and Industry
Kingsgate House, 66-74 Victoria St.
London SW1E 6SW
England
Tel: 0-171-215-5314
Fax: 0-171-215-4366

French Investment Organization
17, Rue Hamelin 75783 Paris Cedex 10
France
Tel: 33-1-44-05-35-07
Fax: 33-1-47-55-65-83

German Investment Development Company
Belvederestr. 40, D-5000 Koln 41
Germany
Tel: 49-221-498-6401
Fax: 49-221-498-6290

Turks and Caicos

The Turks and Caicos are two island groups located in the North Atlantic, southeast of the Bahamas. The Turks consist of two inhabited islands — Grand Turk and Salt Cay, six uninhabited cays, and several "rocks." The Caicos comprise six major islands, the largest of which is Grand Caicos, and several islets. The area of all the islands combined is about 166 square miles (430 square kilometers). In general the islands are flat and low.

The island groups enjoy a tropical marine climate that is moderated by the trade winds. Overall, the climate is dry and sunny. The average annual temperature is about 85 degrees F (29 degrees C). Rainfall averages only about 28 inches (71 centimeters) per year; however, hurricanes are a concern during late spring, summer, and early fall.

About 14,500 people are permanent residents of the Turks and Caicos. Most of the population is descended from Africans, or is of mixed descent. Major religions include Baptist, to which about 41% of the population belongs, Methodist, about 19%, Anglican, 18%, with the rest of the population belonging to various other churches. English is the official language of the islands, and the literacy rate is about 98%. Health care is relatively good, as evidenced by the life expectancy rates: 73 years for men and 77 years for women.

Although many people might be unfamiliar with the Turks and Caicos, the beauty of the islands rivals the finest anywhere. They are quiet and, compared to many of the other islands of the Caribbean, relatively unpopulated. The atmosphere is relaxed. Providenciales — most often referred to simply as Provo — is probably the most popular destination for visitors. Accommodations include everything from resorts and luxury condos to hotels.

Residence Havens

Fine restaurants, nightclubs, a casino, shopping, golf, tennis courts, and an assortment of water sports make the Turks and Caicos a potentially excellent retirement haven.

History and Government

For 900 years before the arrival of the Europeans, the Turks and Caicos were inhabited by the Tainos and Lucayans, native American tribes that migrated from the Orinoco region of South America. While some historians believe that Grand Turk was Columbus's first landfall in 1492, others believe that the islands were discovered by the Spanish explorer Juan Ponce de Leon in 1512. Unfortunately, within a generation after contact with the Europeans, the native Indians of the islands were destroyed through disease and enslavement.

The islands remained uninhabited until 1678 when Bermudians started to develop the salt industry. This led to British control of the islands. In 1799 the Turks and Caicos gained representation in the assembly of the Bahamas, then were annexed to Jamaica in 1973. Today the islands are a dependent territory of the United Kingdom.

The chief of state of the islands is the queen, who appoints, and is represented by, the governor. The governor in turn appoints the chief minister. The legislative branch of government consists of a unicameral Legislative Council that is elected through universal suffrage, starting at 18 years of age. The judicial system of the islands is based on English laws with a small number of laws based on Jamaican and Bahaman laws.

The Economy of the Turks and Caicos

The economy of the islands is based primarily on tourism and offshore financial services. GDP per capita is about U.S.$6,000. The islands have a good infrastructure and financial system to handle the needs of the modern consumer and business person. The U.S. dollar is the official currency of the islands.

Tax Facts of Interest

The Turks and Caicos are considered by many to be one of the best tax havens in the world for several reasons, including:

- There is no income tax.
- There is no tax on capital gains.
- There is no tax on corporate dividends.
- There is no tax on property.
- There is no tax on estates, inheritance, succession, or gifts.
- There is no tax on sales.

Moreover, Britain encourages these tax haven features as an acceptable means of producing revenue for the islands. The Turks and Caicos also possess strong privacy laws, have laws favorable to the formation of offshore corporations, trusts, and financial services companies, and have not entered in to tax treaties with other countries, thus ensuring privacy. Finally, the Turks and Caicos offer a 20 year guarantee against future taxes and guarantee immunity from future fee increases.

Should you be interested in finding out more information about the Turks and Caicos, contact the following:

*Turks and Caicos Islands Tourist Board
Front St.
Cockburn Town, San Salvador
Bahamas
Tel: +242-946-2321
Fax: +242-946-2321*

United Kingdom

The United Kingdom, often referred to as Great Britain, Britain, or England, consists of the island of Great Britain, which includes England, Scotland, and Wales, and the northern one-sixth of the island of Ireland. The total area of the United Kingdom is 94,227 square miles (244,046 square kilometers), or slightly smaller than the area of Oregon. The terrain is mostly low mountains and rugged hills with rolling plains in the east and southeastern part of the England.

The climate of the United Kingdom is temperate. Seasonal temperatures are moderated by a prevailing southwest wind over the North Atlantic Current, giving the lands of the United Kingdom average temperatures that are milder than would seem to be indicated by their latitude. Marked extremes of heat or cold are rare. Average annual temperatures range between 52 degrees F (about 11 degrees C) in the south and 48 degrees F (about 9 degrees C) in the northeast. Average seasonal temperatures vary between an average of about 61 degrees F (16 degrees C) in July to about 40 degrees F (4.5 degrees C) in January. The United Kingdom is known for its mists, fogs, and cloudy days. Indeed, overcast skies are more common than sunshine. Rainfall averages about 30 inches (76 centimeters) annually.

The United Kingdom has a population of about 58,500,000. By far the English are the dominant group, comprising about 81% of the country's population, with the rest being comprised of Scots, 10%, Irish, 2%, Welsh, 2%, Ulster, 2%, with West Indians, Pakistanis, and others accounting for the rest. Because the United Kingdom does not include a question on religion on its census, it is difficult to provide accurate numbers on religion. However, by far the largest religious group in the country is the Anglican Church, followed

Residence Havens

by Roman Catholics, Muslims, Presbyterians, Methodists, Sikhs, Hindus, and Jews. English, of course, is the major language, with Welsh and Scottish also spoken in their respective regions. The literacy rate of the country is 99%.

The standard of living in the United Kingdom is excellent. Health care also is of high quality, evidenced by life expectancy rates of 74 years for men and 79 years for women. Just about any convenience, activity, recreation, or entertainment that one would expect to find in any other advanced country may also be found in the United Kingdom. In addition, the United Kingdom offers a wealth of Anglo-Saxon history, architecture, and English custom. The influence of England on cultures around the world is vast, affecting people around the world. It was Britain that gave the world the likes of King Arthur, Shakespeare, John Locke, Queen Victoria, and Winston Churchill. Many English, Welsh, and Scottish cities and towns offer an atmosphere that can not be found anywhere else in the world.

History and Government

Huge volumes have been written about the history of the United Kingdom. This section is but an overview.

As early as 3,000 B.C. a people known as the Iberians lived in England. It is thought that these were the engineers and builders of spectacular megaliths such as Stonehenge. Between the 8th and 6th centuries B.C., Celtic tribes from the continent swept into the island, forcing most of the Iberians to the northern territories. One of the tribes of Celts was called the Brythons, from whom the name Britain likely derived. For the next several centuries, warring Celts fought each other as well as the remaining Iberians, finally being faced by Julius Caesar and Roman legions in 55 and 54 B.C. It took the Romans over a hundred years to subjugated just a part of Britain. Rome eventually managed to rule much of Britain for more than 400 years, but was never able to conquer the tribes of the north.

When Roman power declined in the 5th century, Britain was invaded by the Germanic tribes of Angles, Saxons, and Jutes. It is from this time that the legends of King Arthur and Camelot come. Some historians believe that Arthur was a Celtic king who defeated the invading Germans, though more legend than fact surrounds this premise. For a short time the Angles became dominant in the "land of the Angles" or "Anglo-Land," which came to be called England.

During the 8th to 10 centuries, England suffered attacks from Scandinavians, known as Vikings. The Vikings plundered and eventually settled along England's shores, in time becoming absorbed in the population.

In 1066, England was invaded for the last time when William the Conqueror of Normandy defeated the English and their king, Harold, at the Battle of Hastings. Within just a few years, William had subjugated virtually all of England under Norman rule. In time, the Normans, like the Vikings before them, were absorbed by the people they conquered.

England of the Middle Ages was a land that struggled with itself and its neighbors. As the rest of the European monarchies grew stronger in absolute power, the English nobility fought to restrain the king's power, culminating in 1215 with the signing of the Magna Carta by King John. This famous writ proved to be the beginnings of England's constitutional government.

By the time Columbus discovered the New World, England was one of the most powerful nations in Europe. That power was soon wielded to establish a colonial empire that extended around the world. Despite the loss of the American colonies after the American war for independence, it was rightfully claimed that the sun never set on the British Empire. British influence around the world was unsurpassed, and today the laws of countless other countries

Residence Havens

are based on British laws. That English is one of the world's major languages is yet another testimony to the reach and dominance of the British Empire.

After the two world wars, British power was severely diminished. With many of its colonies calling for independence, and with its resources spent, Britain granted independence to its colonies, many of whom still remain a part of the Commonwealth of Nations.

Britain's government is officially a constitutional monarchy with the capital at London. Although the queen is the head of state, the head of the government is the prime minister, who is the leader of the party which holds the majority in the House of Commons. The legislative branch of government is a bicameral Parliament: the House of Lords and the House of Commons. Members of the House of Commons are elected by universal suffrage, starting at 18 years of age. Britain's judicial system is based on common laws influenced by early Roman laws. The country is one of the world's great democracies.

The Economy of the United Kingdom

Without question, the United Kingdom is a great trading, commercial, and financial center. Its economy is the fourth largest of Western Europe. Britain has an efficient agriculture sector, significant energy reserves, and a strong financial services sector. Industry, though important to the country's economy, has declined in importance in recent years.

On the whole, Britain's economy is strong. GDP is U.S.$19,500. The currency of Great Britain is the British pound.

Britain's infrastructure is excellent. Numerous sea- and airports are located throughout the country, the nation's highway system is good, and its telecommunications are advanced.

Tax Facts of Interest

Most people don't think of the United Kingdom as being any kind of tax haven. However, within Britain's tax code is the concept of "resident but not domiciled." What this means is that an individual can live in England — reside there in other words — yet not be domiciled there — maintaining his or her permanent home. Thus, this person might maintain his permanent home in another country but reside, or live, in Britain. The key here <u>in the case of "resident but not domiciled"</u> is that an individual so described is taxed only on income that is actually brought into the United Kingdom. As a result, <u>a person can accumulate income earned abroad in offshore accounts and not be taxed on these funds in the United Kingdom</u>.

Because the strategy is somewhat complicated — it's crucial to set up your funds and accounts properly — it is wise to seek the advice of a competent tax expert. It is also essential to monitor Britain's tax laws closely, because the Labor Party has noted that it wishes to tax worldwide income of all residents of the United Kingdom.

Should you be interested in more information about the United Kingdom, contact:

The British Tourist Authority
Thames Tower, Black Rd., Hammersmith
London, England W6 9EL
United Kingdom
Tel: +44-181-846-9000
Fax: +44-181-846-9000

The Embassy of Great Britain
3100 Massachusetts Ave., NW
Washington, DC 20008
Tel: 202-462-1340
Fax: 202-898-4255

The British Tourist Authority
7th Floor
551 Fifth Ave.
New York, NY 10176
Tel: 212-986-2200

The British Tourist Board
40 West 57th St.
New York, NY 10019
Tel: 212-581-4700

The British Tourist Board
210 Clarence St.
Sydney, NSW 2000
Australia
Tel: 2-267-4555

The British Tourist Board
63 Rue Pierre-Charron
75008 Paris
France
Tel: 43-89-11-11

The British Tourist Board
Taunusstrasse 52-60
Frankfurt am Main 1
Germany
Tel: 69-23-80-711

United Kingdom

*The British Tourist Board
Tokyo Club Building
Chiyoda-ku
Tokyo 100
Japan
Tel: 3-3581-3603*

*Scottish Tourist Board
19 Cockspur St.
London SW1Y
United Kingdom
Tel: 0171-930-8661*

*Wales Information Bureau
12 Regent St.
London SW1Y 4PQ
United Kingdom
Tel: 0171-409-0969*

Uruguay

Uruguay is a southern South American country that is located between Argentina to the west and Brazil to the north. On the east and south, Uruguay is bordered by the Atlantic Ocean. A little smaller than the state of Washington, Uruguay is about 68,037 square miles (176,220 square kilometers) in area. Uruguay's topography varies between fertile coastal lowlands, grassy plains in the south, a low plateau in the north and northwest, and low mountains in the east. The country's highest point is Mirado Nacional at 1,644 feet (501 meters).

Uruguay has a warm temperate climate. The average temperature during the warmest months of January and February is about 71 degrees F (22 degrees C), and the average temperature in June, the coldest month, is about 50 degrees F (10 degrees C). Temperatures seldom fall below freezing in any part of the country. Rainfall throughout the country averages about 35 inches (89 centimeters) annually.

About 3,200,000 people live in Uruguay. Most, about 88%, are descended from white Europeans, principally Spanish and Italian. Mestizos make up about 8% of the population, and blacks about 4%. Close to 66% of the population is Roman Catholic. About 4% are Protestants, and another 4% are Jewish. A significant number of people do not belong to any church. Spanish is the predominate language, although Brazilero, a mixture of Portuguese and Spanish, is also spoken along the border with Brazil. The country's literacy rate is 97%. Except for Montevideo, the capital, and other major cities, health care is somewhat limited. Life expectancy is 72 years for men and 78 years for women.

Residence Havens

Although Uruguay is a small country, it has an impressive culture and traditions. Theater, music, and dance are popular pastimes. Art and literature are supported and appreciated. Montevideo is a delightful mix of colonial Spanish, Italian, and Art Deco architecture. Activities and recreational opportunities abound. Restaurants, nightclubs, beach resorts, water sports, yacht and fishing clubs, golf courses, casinos and beautiful homes are found in and around the city. Without doubt, Uruguay is one of the world's least recognized retirement havens.

History and Government

The Charrua Indians were Uruguay's original inhabitants. The first European to encounter them was the Spaniard Juan Diaz de Solis in 1516. The Charrua killed him and most of his party. Subsequent attempts to colonize the territory were repulsed by the Charrua, and it was not until 1624 that the Spanish succeeded in establishing the first permanent settlement on the Rio Negro. During the years of the Colonial Period, Spain and Portugal vied for supremacy in Uruguay with the Spanish finally gaining control in 1777.

In 1814 Uruguayan revolutionaries drove the Spanish governor out of Montevideo, but the new country, called Banda Oriental del Uruguay was too weak to protect its borders. In 1816 the Portuguese in Brazil attacked, completing their conquest in 1821 and annexing the Banda Oriental to Brazil. Uruguayans revolted and reasserted their independence in 1825, with the result being the organization of the Republic of Uruguay in 1830. For the next several years the new country suffered civil wars and violence. Internal struggles continued well into the 20th century with the military often holding the greatest power in the country. This situation continued well into the 1980s.

In recent years Uruguay has prospered under civilian authority. The chief of state and head of the government is the president, who is elected for a five-year term by popular vote. Suffrage is universal and compulsory at 18 years of age. The legislature is composed of a bicameral General Assembly, and the judiciary is based on Spanish civil law.

The Economy of Uruguay

In the past, Uruguay's economy has been hurt by excessive government regulations. High inflation has also undermined growth. During the 1990s, however, the government has taken steps to reduce inflation and reform economic policies, the result being an improving economic climate. Through Mercosur (the Southern Cone Common Market) and the European Union, Uruguay has been exploring avenues through which to expand trade. The country's long-term growth looks promising.

The Uruguayan economy is built around agriculture, meat processing, textiles, leather apparel, tires, petroleum refining, wine, and cement. Much of its exports stem from the agricultural sector. Current GDP per capita is U.S.$7,600. The country's currency is the Uruguayan peso.

Uruguay's infrastructure can best be rated as fair. It's telecommunications system is centered around Montevideo, with facilities declining in quality and reliability as one moves farther from the city. Of the nation's railways, almost half are closed or only partially in operation. Close to 80% of the highways are unpaved. Although providing service, sea- and airports lack modern equipment. Infrastructure modernization poses a major challenge for Uruguay in the upcoming years.

Tax Facts of Interest

Uruguay has numerous taxes, but generally exempts passive income from non-Uruguayan sources paid to a Uruguayan resident. Uruguay is used as a residence haven by many South Americans and Europeans.

it also has free zones, which can be publicly or privately held. All types of industries, trading companies, and service companies are permitted to operate in the free zones. The great incentive here is that <u>any company operating in Uruguayan free zones is exempted from all Uruguayan taxes, present and future, with the exception of contributions to state social security</u>.

For the individual considering future retirement, but who wishes to establish or relocate a business first, Uruguay may be an attractive site.

Should you wish to find out more information about Uruguay, contact the following:

> *The Uruguayan Embassy*
> *1918 F Street, NW*
> *Washington, DC 20006*
> *Tel: 202-331-1313 through 1316*
>
> *U.S. Embassy in Uruguay*
> *Lauro Muller 1776*
> *Montevideo*
> *Mailing Address: APO AA 34035*
> *Tel: 598-2-23-60-61, 48-77-77*
> *Fax: 598-2-48-86-11*

Getting A Second Citizenship

Consideration should be given to the acquisition of more than one passport. The acquisition of multiple passports of course presupposes that you are willing to accept multiple citizenship — and this is not at all a bad idea for many people.

With terrorism on the rise, international travel can be particularly hazardous to citizens of certain countries. Hostage-takers and kidnappers who have commandeered planes and boats have often looked at passports in deciding who shall live and who shall die. A second passport may also give you access to travel in countries where your own passport might not be used because temporary or permanent travel restrictions. If you think this can't happen to you, consider all the Canadians who were refused permission to land in Spain a few years ago during a Spanish-Canadian fishing rights dispute.

For others, the benefits of a second passport may not be quite as pressing, but dual citizenship does nonetheless convey several advantages. Many nations have laws which restrict the purchase of real estate properties. Typically, coastal properties and those in large desirable metropolitan areas are off-limits to foreigners. Such practices have been widespread throughout Europe, Asia, South America — even in Mexico. Paradoxically, some of the available properties have remained unsold for long periods of time, not because they are outrageously priced but rather because locals could not afford to purchase them. The acquisition of a second nationality could be your key to living like a king or queen in one of the world's most desirable cities.

Financial advantages of dual citizenship include the ability to purchase otherwise restricted shares in emerging foreign companies. Many foreign stocks and mutual funds are only available to local citizens. Issuers will require affidavits from potential buyers. Present the appropriate second passport as proof of citizenship and you are home free.

Employment is yet another issue. Foreigners are largely banned from working anywhere outside their own borders. Citizenship in another country can change all of that quickly. In fact many of the world's largest multinational corporations favor employment candidates with dual passports. If you set out to open your own business overseas, the same advantages will apply.

Finally, dual nationality could open all kinds of doors overseas including participation in foreign social security programs, national health programs, even university tuition remission programs. The specific benefits naturally depend on the country you choose.

In most instances, governments only extend citizenship to individuals who have resided within their boundaries for minimum periods ranging from three to five years. These provisions can of course be waived. Few nations are begging for immigrants and those which encourage immigration are selectively looking for individuals who can provide specific services — like physicians, agricultural experts, entrepreneurs likely to create new jobs, and science teachers. After all, what possible benefit can a nation derive from wantonly issuing passports to outsiders with no purpose other than to skirt another nation's laws or to protect the privacy of individuals it hardly knows?

It is possible that you already qualify for a new passport by virtue of your ethnic background. If you are of Germany, Italian, Irish, French, or Jewish ancestry, it is likely that you are eligible. Other countries, however, are eager to naturalize those who do not automatically qualify especially if they can bring professional talent or expertise to their nations. If you have a distinguished career in teaching, engineering, general management, administration, or medicine, you have a decided advantage.

Several international firms claim to have connections which enable them to expedite the passport issuance process, obtaining dual nationalities for their clients in as little as two weeks. Sometimes this can be effected by bribing government bureaucrats, a common and accepted practice in many developing countries. You may be charged $5000 or more for these services with money passing through Swiss banks. Drivers licenses and other documents useful for identification can be obtained in the same fashion. In some cases, completely new identities can be established.

You should be a little wary of such claims. There have been numerous reports of swindles, however, hundreds of clients losing thousands of dollars each year on documents that are never issued. Stories also abound suggesting that some passport acquisition services have simply issued bogus credentials to their clients. If you find yourself in possession of forged travel documents, you could of course end up in prison for many years. Moreover, if the sole purpose of obtaining such documentation is to conceal your identity so that you can commit fraud or some other crime, or to hide a prior criminal record or divorce, you have merely compounded your troubles.

If you choose to pursue dual nationality through legitimate channels, you can probably obtain a valid second passport in a reasonably short time. Be sure to consider any adverse consequences, however. If your are a *naturalized* American citizen, you risk losing your American citizenship by swearing allegiance to another flag, voting in a foreign election, or deliberately renouncing your American citizenship at a U.S. embassy abroad. Native-born Americans will find that their U.S. citizenship is virtually cemented in stone.

You might also be conscripted into the armed services of another nation if you happen to find yourself at the wrong place at the wrong time. Fortunately,

Residence Havens

many nations have moved towards voluntary armies — and if you're as unhealthy as the typical American couch potato, you need not worry anyway.

If you have determined that you don't have a readily available inherited citizenship, and want to pursue the ever changing world of countries that offer nearly instant citizenship to investors, be aware that this will generally cost from $75,000 on up, although a portion of that is usually an investment in government bonds. The countries offering such programs change frequently. The leading expert in such matters is Marshall J. Langer, an American lawyer from Florida, now living in London. He practiced law in Miami for over 30 years before moving to Neuchatel, Switzerland. He has written extensively, lectured, and taught on subjects relating to international and citizenship law. He consults with private clients on matters relating to migration from one country to another, citizenship and passports, residency, and domicile. When you are ready to proceed and want to retain the best talent in such matters, we would recommend that you get in touch with:

Marshall J. Langer, Shutts & Bowen
43 Upper Grosvenor Street
London W1X 9PG, England
Telephone (44 171) 493-4840
Fax (44 171) 493-4299.

Some Examples of Visa-Free Travel & Residence

The person with two or more citizenships, and the ability to engage in visa-free movement because of them, is in a very flexible position. That person has a great deal of protection from oppression by having the ability to pick up and move quickly. At the point that citizens of some particular country might be unable to travel, either because of domestic or foreign restrictions, the person with dual nationality will be protected and can always go to his second country — or to any country that allows visa-free entry to the citizens of that second country.

There are actually two levels of visa-free status, depending upon the exact countries involved.

The first is the tourist or business travel level, which allows relative freedom of movement but not the freedom to settle. This level is also the most easily revoked, as in the 1995 example of Canadian tourists being banned from entering Spain during a dispute over fishing rights.

The second level of visa-free status is that which confers some right of residence and work. The prime example of course is having a citizenship of a European Union country, which gives one the right to live and work in any other European Union country. (This right covers more geography than one might at first expect, including the French departments of Reunion, Guadeloupe, and Martinique for example.)

In terms of freedom of movement, the Latin American zone now has freedom of movement and work between Paraguay, Uruguay, Brazil and Argentina, with Chile to soon be included.

The Caricom countries of the Caribbean have a more limited right for technical and executive personnel to live and work in other member countries.

NAFTA gives a similar, but even more limited, right to move between Mexico, the United States, and Canada for those who are engaged in business in one of the member countries.

Having a second citizenship in any of these groupings creates the ability to live a semi-nomadic and often tax-free life. Staying less than 6 months in each of one's countries (perhaps locations of business interests, branch offices, or just second homes) will often be sufficient to escape all income taxes. (Even Americans can get some limited benefits, since a bona-fide foreign residence lets a U.S. citizen exclude $70,000 per year in earned income, despite the U.S. being the only major country to tax based upon citizenship rather than residence.)

Why Your Investments Also Need To Reside In A Haven

Once you are living a international lifestyle, or living in a residence haven, if not before, it helps to find a haven for your personal investments — bank accounts, mutual funds, unit trusts, annuities, etc. There are great advantages in creating a personal or family trust in an offshore tax haven or money management center. Having all of ones finances managed by professional offshore managers provides a great deal of privacy, and the ability to have somebody qualified and able to act on your behalf immediately in case of an emergency. And it is useful to put your money management on autopilot and concentrate on doing the things that you want to do, not to mention that 99% of the time professional fund managers will do a better job than you can. Another reason is that the your assets can pass privately to his heirs without the interference of government probate systems, or forced inheritance laws in the country where the bank accounts or investment portfolios are held. For Americans, offshore structures become particularly important for protection against lawsuits, and sometimes government forfeitures. Unfortunately, many other countries are following this American trend, so people from anywhere would do well to plan to have their offshore structures in place before there is a need. After all, you aren't disappointed if you buy fire insurance and your house doesn't burn down. Placing your investments in a proper structure plays the same role.

Tax havens truly become an important key for an investor who has any form of active business involvement — from something as limited as collecting copyright or patent royalties all the way up to a very active business. A tax haven company provides the permanent base that any company needs to deal with the world at large, since a company cannot effectively become portable and continue to do business. The tax haven company becomes the investor's interface between his personal lifestyle and the need to anchor the business somewhere and have it appear conventional to those it does business with.

The royalty earning investor may use a tax haven company to take advantage of treaties that eliminate the withholding taxes in the high-tax countries, and then the tax haven company can funnel the money tax free to the investor.

An investor with more active business involvements may use a company in a different type of tax haven — perhaps to publish a newsletter sold on a worldwide basis, or to own a fishing trawler working the high seas, or just as a place to register his personal yacht.

Solving The Worldwide Taxation Problem For American Citizens

American readers of offshore books are usually faced with the frustrating fact that much of what is said does not apply to them, because the U.S. taxes its citizens on a worldwide basis regardless of where they reside. Much of this problem can be solved with combinations of trusts and corporations, of the type of tax planning that The Harris Organization does for its clients (see the sections on forming trusts and corporations for more details). But this still leaves the American taxpayer struggling through the various hoops of the tax code to protect his wealth from taxation.

Many publications talk about the value of offshore techniques to defer taxes. Creation of an offshore business by an American citizen will generally defer taxation until dividends are paid, allowing untaxed profits to compound in the foreign corporation.

This "option strategy" also works for inheritance taxes. With proper tax planning, one can create a large estate, and if one renounces U.S. citizenship before death, that entire estate can pass tax free to ones heirs. Thus a person is able to maintain and use their U.S. citizenship for a lifetime, and then take the option of renunciation of citizenship when it is no longer relevant — perhaps when living in an overseas retirement haven. All of the residential tax havens just discussed become very suitable for an American pursuing this strategy.

The same strategy is effective for a non-U.S. citizen who has been a U.S. permanent resident for a number of years and then leaves the U.S. This allows a person to work in the U.S. and accumulate wealth, while their accumulated savings out of the U.S. tax free when they cease being resident.

Sources of Help for Offshore Investing

There seems to be a tendency in some circles to look for offshore financial institutions that will deal anonymously, or let you use a false name. But do you really want to entrust your funds to an institution that doesn't care who it does business with? A bank that will give its Visa card to Mr. Anonymous? That's not a very safe depository, is it? None of the institutions on my recommended list will deal that way. They will want, and will check, references, and they want to deal only with persons of substance.

Britannia Corporate Management Limited

Another business specializing in the formation of offshore corporations and trusts is Britannia Corporate Management Limited, located in the Cayman

Islands. Its president, Gary F. Oakley, is a Canadian with over 18 years of Cayman Islands residency. Britannia is licensed to manage investment holding and trading companies, real estate holding companies, patent holding companies, and insurance holding companies. It is licensed to incorporate and manage corporations registered in the Cayman Islands. As such, the firm can service as the registered office of a corporation, provide its secretary, officers and directors, or undertake any day-to-day functions that may be required. More information can be obtained by writing the following:

> *Britannia Corporate Management Limited*
> *Attn: New Clients Information*
> *P. O. Box 1968*
> *Whitewall Estates, Grand Cayman*
> *Cayman Islands*

Britannia can be reached by fax at +1 345 949 0716, directing your communication to New Clients Information.

Lines Overseas Management Services

For asset management and securities brokerage, Lines Overseas Management Services is one of the most respected businesses operating today. Notable is its independence from onshore influences. It does not have a parent company controlling it from a big country, and does not maintain subsidiaries. Lines Overseas Management clears its trades locally, leaving no paper trail on its client activities in New York, London, or elsewhere.

Rates on certificates of deposit and liquid accounts offered through Lines are generally higher than those available in other markets. The firm offers proprietary Visa Gold debit cards to access cash on deposit. Offshore asset managers are appointed to provide personalized service in the selection of investments in order to best meet specific client needs. These managers fully understand the investment and tax avoidance objectives of overseas customers.

Lines is clearly not for everyone, however. It only accepts accounts with US $250,000 minimums. One of its offshore asset managers has been widely recognized in best-selling books and periodicals. He is Scott Oliver, a British subject, who earlier helped to develop sophisticated trading systems for some of Wall Street's largest investment banks. Today, many American estate planning attorneys refer their wealthiest clients to Oliver for financial advice. He has broad familiarity and expertise not only with publicly-traded issues of all kinds, but has a strong track record in private placements.

For more information, contact the following:

> *Mr. Scott Oliver*
> *Offshore Asset Manager*
> *Lines Overseas Management (Cayman) Ltd.*
> *P.O. Box 1159GT, Genesis Building*
> *Grand Cayman, Cayman Islands*

Mr. Oliver can be reached by telephone at +1 345 949-5808 or by fax at +1 345 949-1338.

Skye Fiduciary Services Limited

Skye Fiduciary Services Limited are among the foremost experts in offshore planning. Under the direction of its chairman Charles Cain, formerly managing director of the second merchant bank to open in the Isle of Man, Skye Fiduciary is the most experienced offshore corporate and trust management business in the jurisdiction. Although Skye offers a full range of company and trust management services, their expertise in designing novel company structures to meet the needs of foreign clients is unique.

For further information, write the following:

Residence Havens

> Skye Fiduciary Services Limited
> Attn: New Clients Department
> 2 Water Street
> Ramsey, Isle of Man 1M8 1JP
> United Kingdom

Their telephone number is +44 1624 816117. Fax service is available at +44 1624 816645; direct communications to New Clients Information.

JML Swiss Investment Counsellors

One of the leaders in Swiss financial management is JML Swiss Investment Counsellors, a firm which offers a unique style of financial management. Clients can customize and control their own portfolios and still receive comprehensive management advice from some of the world's best experts on financial matters.

Recognizing that investors have differing goals, time frames, and tolerance for risk, JML's managers work with their individual clients to help them target their unique objectives. This naturally requires continued surveillance and analysis of worldwide economic trends, political events, financial markets, currencies, and other factors which could make some investments particularly attractive and others most unfavorable. Few individuals have the time or expertise to undertake this kind of evaluation themselves.

Further information about JML can be obtained by writing the following:

> *Weber Hartmann Vrijhof & Partners Ltd.*
> *Zurichstrasse 110b*
> *CH-8134 Adliswil*
> *Switzerland*
> *Telephone +41 1 709 1115*
> Fax +41 1 709 1113

Why Your Investments Also Need to Reside in a Haven

Their telephone number is (41) 41 726 5500 and their fax number is (41) 41 726 5590, Attention Department 212.

Weber Hartmann Vrijhof & Partners

Potential investors may also want to consider the expertise of Weber Hartmann Vrijhof & Partners, another independent Swiss portfolio management firm. The principals of this partnership, former bankers and portfolio managers, provide services to individuals, offshore trusts, and corporations in need of investment advice.

The minimum opening portfolio to be managed by this firm is $200,000 or equivalent. The management team here normally recommends that a portion of the portfolio be invested in hard currencies other than the U.S. dollar including the Swiss franc, French franc, German mark, and Dutch guilder. Respected for their conservative approach to portfolio management, the partners have recently invested heavily in short-term bonds and have achieved double-digit yields for their clients in 1995 and 1996.

For more information, you can write to the following:

Weber Hartmann Vrijhof & Partners Ltd.
Attn: New Clients Department
Zurichshstrasse 110B
8134 Adllswil, Switzerland

Their telephone number is (41-1) 709-11-15 and their fax number (41-1) 709-11-13, Attention New Clients Department.

Dunn & Hargitt International Group

Recently, many international investors have become dissatisfied with the small annual return on Euro-dollar deposits.

This is why private and institutional investors throughout the world are looking at other areas where returns can be in the area of 20-25% a year, to help offset the high annual rates of inflation on luxury goods.

The Dunn & Hargitt International Group, founded in 1961, has specialized in doing research for developing Portfolio Management Programs that have the potential of providing investors with a high return on their capital by investing in a diversified portfolio trading in the commodity, currency, precious metals, and financial futures markets in the United States and throughout the world.

The Dunn & Hargitt group offers investors the possibilitiy of participating in several of the different pools that are managed by them by investing through the investment programs that are offered by their affiliate, Winchester Life in Gibraltar, but which are actually managed by The Dunn & Hargitt International Group.

At the time of publication they are offering three possible investment alternatives, including The Winchester Life Umbrella Account (which allows 100% of a client's money to be invested in a diversified futures portfolio), The Winchester Life 100% Guaranteed Investment Account (in which Lloyds Bank acts as custodian trustee and US Government Zero Coupon Treasury Bonds are set aside to guarantee the client's capital), and The Winchester Life 150% Guaranteed Investment Account (which is a similar program, but guaranteeing that the client will receive at least 150% of the value deposited with a maturity date at least ten years in the future).

The average net return for the 150% Guaranteed Investment Account over the last six years would have been 22% a year. The average net return on the 100% Guaranteed Investment Account over the last six years would have been 27% a year. The average annual net return for The Winchester Life Umbrella Account over the last twelve years would have been 35% a year.

Why Your Investments Also Need to Reside in a Haven

The minimum accounts accepted are $20,000 for The Winchester Life Umbrella Account, $20,000 for The Winchester Life 100% Guaranteed Account, and $50,000 for The Winchester Life 150% Guaranteed Account.

Although commodities are a speculative form of investment, investors everywhere are diversifying part of their portfolios to take part in the considerable potential profit opportunities that are available in the commodity, currency, precious metals and financial futures markets. The programs devised by the Dunn & Hargitt International Group will make profits if significant trends develop in either direction; i.e. up or down. This does not mean that short term results are always profitable, however the Dunn & Hargitt proven trading systems can provide above average returns over the longer term. Their objective is to make a profit for their clients of between 20% and 40% per annum and their computer trading systems are geared to this level of performance.

For more information, contact:

The Dunn & Hargitt International Group
c/o Dunn & Hargitt Research S.A.
Department S-697
The Dunn & Hargitt Building
41 av. Legrand, box 1
1050 Brussels
Belgium
Tel: +32 2 640 3280
Fax: +32 2 640 4628; attn: Dept. S-697

The structure of the Dunn & Hargitt Group has been established so that no taxes are withheld from the client's investment on the international commodity, currency, precious metals and financial futures markets. Because of this they can only manage money for investors who are neither citizens nor residents of the United States.

The Dunn & Hargitt International Group offers complete confidentiality to all of its clients, and will not reveal any information on a client or on its accounts to any third parties.

Tax-Free Investing in the United States

Few Americans realize this, but the United States is considered a tax haven by many foreign investors. While U.S. citizens are struggling with federal, state, and local tax burdens of 40% or more of their total income, foreign investors often can invest in the United States tax-free or almost tax-free.

The country is not a straightforward no-tax haven like the Cayman Islands or the Bahamas. Instead, it has some complicated tax laws and tax treaties that, when taken together and fully understood, provide opportunities for the foreign investor to make low-tax gains in U.S. investments.

The United States encourages tax-free foreign investment because it needs foreign capital to finance the economy and the government budget deficit. For example, Congress generally imposes a 30% withholding tax on all interest payments to foreign residents and corporations. Foreign investors let it be known quickly that they would take their money elsewhere if the withholding tax remained, however, and exceptions to the tax now exist.

The great benefit of the U.S. tax haven for many foreigners occurs when the U.S. tax rules are combined with those of other countries. The United States taxes its citizens and residents on their worldwide income. But noncitizens and nonresidents are not taxed on income from certain sources within this country. As a result, there are a number of foreign individuals who invest in the U.S. in order to take advantage of these non-taxable situations.

As a nonresident alien, you can get these benefits in many situations:

- No U.S. taxes on bank-deposit interest

Residence Havens

- No U.S. tax on capital gains earned on U.S. stocks and bonds.

There will, however, be some tax on dividends from U.S. stocks.

In cases in which a tax might be incurred, such as on dividends, this often can be reduced or avoided by locating an offshore corporation in a country that has a favorable tax treaty with the United States. The Treasury Department has renegotiated a number of the tax treaties, but there still are some under which the U.S. withholding tax rate on dividends is significantly reduced.

Investing in U.S. real estate used to be an easy way to tax-free income and gains for nonresident aliens. But the rules were changed in 1980, and the profits no longer will be tax-free.

American Options Investing

Since capital gains are generally not taxable to foreigners, obviously any investing program which makes its profits in the form of capital gains, rather than dividends, interest or other types of earnings, is highly desirable. Unfortunately, there are not many such investing programs.

But one that does exist is trading options on stocks or on a stock index (such as the Standard & Poor's 500 Index). Since the gain or loss from trading in options is a capital gain, any profits made by a foreigner from trading in such options are free from any tax imposed by the United States.

As many investors already know, options are notoriously speculative and most people who try trading in them wind up losing money. Therefore, in order to take advantage of this tax benefit, it is first imperative to find a method of trading options which has a good probability of actually making money.

Almost any method of trading options which has the chance of making an above average return also carries a commensurate high degree of risk. But some practitioners of the arcane art of options trading do manage to do better

Tax-Free Investing in the United States

than others over the years. One such person who has done very well for his clients is Max G. Ansbacher, Chairman of Ansbacher Investment Management, Inc., located in the prestigious Rockefeller Center complex in New York City.

Mr. Ansbacher has a long and distinguished involvement with options. In fact, he is the author of the first book published on the modern form of options, titled *The New Options Market, Revised and Enlarged Edition*. It was originally written in 1975 and Mr. Ansbacher has been trading options professionally ever since. In addition to this book, which has become one of the all time best selling books on options, he has written two other books on investing, has lectured on options at over 50 investment conferences in both the U.S. and overseas, and is the creator of The Ansbacher Index which is broadcast over the world wide facilities of the CNBC cable network.

He manages accounts for investors in both the U.S. and overseas. What sets Mr. Ansbacher apart from many others is that he has an excellent record of bringing in above average profits for his clients. Since most people who buy options seem to lose money, we asked Mr. Ansbacher what the key was to his success. He replied, "Yes, I agree that most people who buy options do seem to lose money. But what many people don't realize is that the money which the options buyers lose, doesn't disappear from the face of the earth. Rather it becomes the profits of the options *sellers*. And therefore, I concentrate in *selling* options."

What Mr. Ansbacher was saying is that options trading is actually a zero sum game when one looks at the total overall economic effect. This means that buying and selling options in its total impact on the economy does not either create any money or lose any money (except transaction costs). If the sellers make money, the buyers lose money. And if the buyers make money, then the sellers must lose money.

Since the options *buyers* tend to be the ones who lose money, it therefore must be true that the options *sellers* are the ones who make money over the long run. We asked Mr. Ansbacher why this should be true. His answer was, "The options buyers tend to be less sophisticated than the sellers. They don't always carefully assess the chances that their stocks will really go up enough to make money when they buy a call. Similarly, if people think a stock or a stock market is going to go down, they often over estimate how much it is going to go down. They will buy a put which is going to lose money unless the stock makes a really unusually large move within a relatively short period of time. These are the options I sell."

Of course there is not an investment program yet invented which makes money on every single trade, and option selling is no exception. When we asked Mr. Ansbacher about this, he said, "Certainly there are times when we have losses, but we believe that the probability lies with the sellers. And so we usually find that every loss is matched by many more winners."

Selling options is something which has to be done very carefully, because the risk is high. We asked Mr. Ansbacher what he does to control this risk. He said that the first defense was to control the number of options which he sells. "I usually sell only about one fifth the number of options which margin rules permit me to do. The second line of defense is that I use stop loss orders, which in most instances will automatically get me out of the options before the losses rise to a point which I consider unacceptable."

He continued, "The most interesting line of defense and the most important from the point of view of making money, is that I sell out-of-the-money options. This means that I sell options which have a strike price which is a distance away from the current price of the underlying security." We should point out that a strike price is the level at which an option becomes effective.

What Mr. Ansbacher means is that if a stock is 100, for example, he will not sell the 100 strike price call, because it is tool likely that the stock will go above 100 and he might lose money. Instead, he might sell the call with a strike price of 120. The stock would have to be above 120 at the option's expiration for the seller of the option to sustain a loss. Obviously it is less likely that a stock will go up 20 points than it will merely go up a few points. So, by selling out-of-the-money options, Mr. Ansbacher is able to shift the probabilities in his favor.

Another major decision which an options trader has to make is whether to be trading calls, which go up in price when a stock goes up, or puts which go up in price when the stock goes down. Mr. Ansbacher said that he makes this decision based upon a number of factors, including his long experience in the field. "One of the factors I rely upon, is my own Ansbacher Index. This Index tells me whether the puts or the calls are higher priced. Since I am selling these options, I will generally choose to sell the ones which are higher priced. I believe the Index also gives an indication of which way the stock market is likely to go in the intermediate future." Thus, Mr. Ansbacher can sell options on the stock market which will be profitable for his clients if the market moves as The Ansbacher Index indicates it is likely to do.

The minimum account which Mr. Ansbacher accepts is US$100,000, and he accepts accounts from people residing anywhere in the world. Depending upon the type of account, the investor will receive monthly or quarterly statements giving the exact value of the account. Clients are encouraged to discuss their accounts personally with Mr. Ansbacher.

For more information contact:

Ansbacher Investment Management, Inc.
Attn: New Clients Information
45 Rockefeller Plaza, 20th Floor
New York NY 10111
telephone: (212) 332-3280
fax: (212) 332-3283; Attn: New Clients Information

Asset Allocation — The Key To Successful Investing

One of the newest forms of investments in America is called asset allocation. Basically what it means is that one investment is "allocated" to a number of different types of investments by a professional investment allocator. The reason for this allocation is that no one type of investment is the best in all investment climates, and no one type of investment is usually appropriate for all of one person's investment money.

By using an asset allocation program, a person can invest a large amount of his principal in one place, gaining ease of tracking the investment, while attaining the advantage of having a number of different investments to serve his different investment objectives.

The asset allocator performs the service for the investor of allocating varying amounts of a total investment into different areas of investing, such as income stocks, growth stocks, small capitalization stocks, etc., and a variety of fixed income securities.

For modest to medium-sized investments, one method of attaining even more diversification of investments, and expertise in the actual details of the investments, is to allocate the investment among various top-rated mutual funds. As is well known, mutual funds can perform a number of important tasks for the investor. Diversification among a large number of stocks is possible for even a relatively small sum of money. Expertise is available on any type of investment at a relatively low price. Last, there is great liquidity with ease of purchasing and selling.

The actual allocation into different mutual funds will depend upon three principal criteria:

1 What is the risk to reward profile of the individual investor,

2 What is the need of the investor for predictable current income as opposed to the desire for capital gains, and

3 What is the state of the economic and investment cycles at the particular moment in time.

The first and most important criteria are clearly the needs of the investor. These outweigh any thoughts of where any market may be going or where an allocator believes that the most money can be made. The first need which needs to be addressed is the risk which the investor is prepared to accept. All investment involves some degree of risk, but that risk can rage from the minor risk of how inflation can impact an investment in the next 90 days, to the risk of a high flying initial public offering in a company which may have no earnings and no prospect for earnings in the foreseeable future.

The amount of risk which is appropriate for an individual investor depends upon both the investors actual economic situation and his psychological attitudes towards risk of loss. Human temperament plays a very large role in determining risk tolerance. For example, if a person remembers a period of his or her past where they did not have enough money to make ends meet, they may be very adverse to taking any risk at all. Their attitude may be, "We worked hard for that money, and we don't want to lose it."

Others may have almost the opposite approach. They may never have known deprivation, and may have earned a good income all their life. Their attitude may be that they can live very well on their current earnings, and so any savings can be used to speculate. If the speculation turns out to be successful, that will be great and they can raise their standard of living even further. But if the speculation doesn't work out, that's OK too because they will simply continue living as they have.

Thus a good investment allocator will first determine what the needs of his clients are with respect to risk. One method is to determine first how much money is needed to maintain the current standard of living of the investor, and if he or she is not yet retired, how much of the investment will be needed when they do retire. Whatever amount is needed for these purposes is then designated as income producing principal and is invested accordingly into low-risk, high-yielding investments.

The balance can then be invested according to the investor's wishes into areas which can offer the promise of large capital gains in the future. This is the risk portion of the principal, and care must be taken so that the allocator and the investor agree on what amount of risk is to be taken.

The third and equally important task of allocating is to attempt to maximize the return to the investor from the changes in the economic cycle. When business has been in a slump and starts to turn up with both interest rates and inflation low, the largest profits are typically made in the stock market. But as the economy continues to expand, interest rates will rise and so will inflation. These factors make the prognosis for the economy less rosy, and the stock market may start to gyrate, and then fall. Perhaps gently at first and then more rapidly. So the stock market is definitely not the place to be.

At the same time that the stock market is suffering from inflation, the price of hard assets such as gold, oil, and real estate could well be rising rapidly. It is in these areas that fortunes are made during inflationary periods in the economy.

And then as the economy finally begins to cool down due to the effect of high interest rates, interest rates will begin to fall nd the big money may be made by investing in long-term non-callable bonds.

Thus a good allocator must keep in mind the needs of the individual investor and the current status of the economy. And of course he must have an intimate familiarity with specific investments which are available to investors. Whether they be stocks, bonds, or fixed income securities, the allocator must know which are appropriate for the investor and which will likely do well in the present stage of the economy.

Our favorite allocator is Max G. Ansbacher, a man who has been a practicing lawyer and is still licensed to practice law. He has had over twenty years' experience with stocks and stock markets. He is the man we recommend for options in the section above, and his credentials in the stock market are equally impressive. The second book he wrote is titled *How to Profit from the Coming Bull Market* and it was published in the summer of 1981 near the bottom of the long bear market which had actually begun in 1973.

This book explained how and why a strong bull market was about to start on Wall Street. At the time it was published the book was largely ignored by a public which had grown cynical about a stock market which seemed to do nothing but go sideways or down, year after year.

But just one year after Mr. Ansbacher's book was published, the market suddenly took off like a rocket in August 1982 to start one of its greatest bull markets ever, and to establish Mr. Ansbacher's reputation as an insightful student of the stock market. Today Mr. Ansbacher heads up his own firm, Ansbacher Investment Management, Inc., located in Rockefeller Center, New York City.

We recently asked Mr. Ansbacher what his philosophy was concerning asset allocation. He replied, "Asset allocation is probably the most important single aspect of any investment program. And yet what is so strange about it is that it is often not even considered by investors. Some people will have most of their money in the stock market most of the time, unaware of the large risks which the market sometimes contains. Others believe in bonds, and continue to invest most or all of their money there, apparently unaware that in the 1970's and early 1980's the bond market was the biggest money loser of any investment. I would say that asset allocation is not just important, it is the key to successful investing."

In view of the importance which asset allocation has, we wondered just how Mr. Ansbacher went about handling an asset allocation account for a client. "The first thing I do is to talk to the client in whatever depth is necessary to determine the proper risk profile for the client. This depends upon his current financial situation and what he foresees for his future situation as well as his psychological feelings towards money and the potential loss of money. The second thing I do is to make an outline of the client's need for current income. This naturally has a great deal of influence on how we can invest the funds."

"Only after this has been done, do I then discuss with the client where I think the financial markets are heading and where the best returns are likely to be made in the future. The first step in actually making the investments are to decide upon the proportion of money going into each class of investments. The second part is to select the actual investments. For a number of reasons, I select from among the thousands of mutual funds which are available in the U.S. They range all the way from bond to preferred stocks, to common stocks of all types. There is usually a time and a place for almost all of them, but we try to pick the best one for that particular client at that particular time in the client's life, and in the life of the markets."

Mr. Ansbacher explained that his minimum investment is $100,000, and that he works with some of the biggest mutual fund organizations in the U.S., including Fidelity, Dreyfus and other mutual fund management firms. He does not bill his clients for a fee or commission for the work he does, because his compensation is paid to him by the mutual funds.

We have always believed that to be a good asset allocator is one of the most difficult tasks in the investment world, because it requires so many different considerations. To see just what kind of factors Mr. Ansbacher considers we asked him how he would go about planning an asset allocation program for a client whom we made up.

We gave him as an example of a potential client, a 50-year-old German married man who earns the equivalent of $200,000 a year and has a well-funded pension plan with his company. He is in good health and plans to retire at about the age of 65. We asked Mr. Ansbacher to assume that this man comes to him with $300,000 to invest. Here is how Mr. Ansbacher went about making his asset allocation process.

Mr. Ansbacher thought out loud, "The first question I have is about the amount of $300,000. Since he has a pension plan with his company, it is obviously not pension money. It is also a rather large amount for a person earning $200,000 to want to invest in the U.S. Is it inherited money? Does his wife earn money? Is this his life savings? Did he make a successful investment? The reason I ask this question is that it is very important to know if the money is replaceable. If it is inherited, will there be more to follow, or is this all? First I would want to know whether there will be more money coming in or not."

"Second, I would want to know more about his potential future obligations. Do he or his wife having living parents or other relatives who may need financial support in the future? How much support, if any, does he expect that his children will need in the future? Does he have disability insurance or a company plan in case he becomes disabled before he retires? Is there some specific financial goal that he has, such as acquiring a vacation home, yacht or other item which will require a substantial amount of ready cash. All these factors related to the amount of risk which I would want to take."

"The next set of considerations center around his financial situation now. Since he lives in Germany, this means that he pays a high tax on income such as dividends and interest, but pays no capital gains tax. Right away that sways me into investments which are likely to have high capital gains. I would want to know whether the $200,000 he earns covers all of his current expenses, or whether his current standard of living is so high that he needs extra income each year."

"Once we have the answers to these questions, we can begin to solve the problem of how best to allocate this investment. If there are no likely financial needs coming up in the future, and if at the time of the investment I decide that the stock market is not over priced or likely to decline for other reasons, I would place most of the money into various stock funds. I am particularly fond of funds which use value investing, which means that they pick stocks based upon how large an amount of earnings one gets for each dollar invested. This is another way of saying that they seek out stocks with high quality and low price/earnings ratios."

"The reason I like value investing is that many studies have shown that low price/earnings stocks outperform other stocks in normal markets. And in down markets heir inherent value keeps them from falling as far as others. The second group of stocks I would pick would be senior growth stocks. This means stocks which grow year after year because they are gaining market share, or because they are in a solid growth industry. Examples of this are some pharmaceutical companies which are constantly creating new and better drugs, or highly efficient national retail chains which are constantly gaining market share over local competitors."

"One advantage which growth stocks have for this particular client is that they usually don't pay a very large dividend, which fits right in which his local tax structure. Depending upon the wishes of the client, we would consider some gold stocks as a hedge against inflation. And we might add some mutual funds which specialize in large capitalization companies, because these are the tried and proven winners among all the competition in the economy, and often outperform other stocks when the economy softens."

"I would also place a portion of the assets into a short or medium term bond fund for three reasons:

1 This could be a source of money in case an emergency arose which required a withdrawal from the fund,

2 It is a reserve in case some outstanding bargains come up for investment, and

3 It is a hedge against a downturn in the stock market."

Of course the actual percentage allocations would be discussed with the client. The actual funds selected would depend upon their performance records at the time of the investment. And in general, much of the allocation would depend upon the state of the economy at the time of the investment."

We thanked Mr. Ansbacher for sharing his thoughts with us, and for giving us an inside look at how he goes about this critically important task. We believe that he is one of the very best people working with investors to achieve their personal financial goals, through custom tailoring an investment allocation to their personal needs. Investors interested in using his services can contact him as follows:

Ansbacher Investment Management, Inc.
Attn: New Clients Information
45 Rockefeller Plaza, 20th Floor
New York NY 10111
telephone: (212) 332-3280
fax: (212) 332-3283; Attn: New Clients Information

Using Canada as a Stepping Stone

At the outset we warn you the tax reduction suggestions contained in this exclusive report may sound radical to the less adventurous reader. However drastic, you can be certain the steps recommended here are legal and the ultimate financial goals attainable - for those willing to do what is necessary.

The rewards for the bold and brave include five years free of tax obligations - and much lower taxes in the years beyond. The sacrifice required may be the renunciation of your United States citizenship, but in exchange you get the solid prospect of a lifetime with little or no taxes - with assured protection for your assets - and with expanded future income and accumulated personal wealth.

The key to this almost tax-free existence is found in the right combination of exceptional Canadian statutory tax breaks available right now for new immigrants - together with your own careful structuring of personal, corporate and family finances on an international scale.

Read on and discover a whole new concept of tax saving and asset protection, perhaps not for the faint-hearted - but certainly for the wise and wealthy.

Canada - Number One in the World

In 1992 when leading economists at United Nations headquarters in New York researched and published an international guide to the best nations

Residence Havens

in which to live and work, Canada was judged "number one." (Japan came in second, the United States only sixth and in tenth place was merry olde England).

The factors used in making this surprising choice (to Americans, perhaps) encompassed Canada's high standard of living; minimal class divisions; low crime rates with a high sense of individual personal security; the clean environment, air and water; beautiful scenery and wide open spaces; many and varied economic opportunities; ample government support services; extensive infrastructure; comprehensive shopping and sports facilities; available and affordable housing; and the generous hospitality of the Canadian people.

Even with long harsh winters, a continuing bi-lingual, English-French problem and long-standing separatist political sentiment in the province of Quebec, on balance the UN officials found Canada to be the most attractive nation in the world.

The virtues of Canada as the place to live are known around the world, if the number of recent immigrants is any indicator.

In 1993, for example, Canada's population of 29.2 million - projected to peak at about 31 million by 2026 - was increased by 240,138 new citizens. Canada, a modern nation built by European settlers, has increased its flow of immigrants by three-fold since 1985, a year when total population was 25 million and only 85,000 new citizens arrived. Since then increasing numbers have been admitted including many wealthy Asians, especially residents of Hong Kong, the British crown colony slated for Communist China's take over in 1997. The top ten national sources of immigrants since 1986 have been the United States, India, Vietnam, Poland, the United Kingdom, the Philippines, Guyana, and El Salvador.

Canada now has the highest per capita immigration rate of any industrialized nation in the world, an in-flux that has caused widespread public demand for limiting further immigration. A May 1995 national poll showed

234

three out of five Canadians favoring a five-year moratorium on all new immigration.

Reflecting the trend towards tough new immigration controls in most western European nations - and similar demands in the U.S. - Canada's government adopted a scaled-down 1995 immigration quota in the range of 190,00 to 215,000, well below recent annual quotas of 230,000.

But don't let this anti-immigration sentiment concern you. As you will learn in a moment, you may qualify as just the type of new citizen Canada welcomes with open arms.

Tax Free New Canadians

About Canadian Taxes

Before we get to the good news - the big tax break for new Canadian immigrants - you should know that the tax system of Canada is tough and comprehensive, imposing burdensome tax rates on the income of individual taxpayers (over 50 percent), and corporations (up to 45 percent). In 1994 writing in the Wall Street Journal, economist Alan Reynolds of the Hudson Institute in Indianapolis offered the opinion that "Canada is being taxed to death," citing high income and corporate taxes as well as a seven percent federal sales tax piled on top of similar provincial taxes.

But there is one very attractive feature of Canadian taxation policy; unlike the United States, Canada does not tax the worldwide income or foreign assets of its non-resident citizens living abroad. Canada taxes only the worldwide income of its residents - citizens and resident aliens alike - who live in Canada at any time during the calendar year. A "resident" by law includes individuals, corporations and trusts located in Canada.

Residence Havens

Non-resident Canadians, wherever they live, are taxed on income sources within the country, and on business and other capital assets if taxable transactions occur within Canada. Canadian citizens employed abroad, even for extended periods of time, are liable for some limited domestic income taxes, though double taxation credits are permitted when foreign taxes are paid.

Enjoying Life Tax Free

However tough Canadian taxes may be for the average native-born citizen living in Canada's eleven provinces and two territories, there exists a huge loophole available only to wealthy new immigrants. This major tax saving was deliberately written into law in order to encourage new arrivals with financial means.

And it is this Canadian preference for new citizens with substantial investment capital that can translate into huge tax savings and far-reaching financial gains for you and your business.

Here's why:

- A qualified immigrant accepted for eventual Canadian citizenship is eligible for a complete personal income tax moratorium for the first five calendar years of residence in Canada - zero taxes if the source of your income is an offshore, non-Canadian trust or corporation - either or both of which you can easily create before you move to Canada and become a citizen.

As a general rule, Canada has a three year residence requirement after immigrant admission before citizenship is granted, but a five year residence is required in order to be eligible for this very special tax break.

- Canadian citizens and resident aliens employed by certain statutorily-recognized "international financial centers," such as the major one that has been developed in Montreal, are forgiven 50 percent of all federal and provincial income taxes as long as they are employed by one of the qualified companies that are a part of the center.

Generally combined federal/provincial income and social security taxes average one third of gross salary, so this specialized employment earns a substantial tax saving.

- Much "offshore" or foreign source income, dividends and interest paid to Canadian citizens, new or old, can be sheltered from immediate income or other taxes, especially if payments come from qualified foreign trusts or "affiliated corporations" as recognized by Canadian revenue laws.

- Unlike the U.S. with its top rate of 55 percent estate taxes, Canada has abolished all death taxes. The heirs of wealthy Americans with an estate of $3 million or more pay 55 percent of the estate value - and can pay as much as 60 percent in total U.S. federal death taxes. Even the estates of Americans who die leaving as little as $600,000 pay 37 percent in death taxes. State estate taxes and probate fees are added to these hefty U.S. sums.

In sharp contrast, Canadians pay no estate taxes. The federal estate tax was abolished in 1971, with the provinces following suit until the last death tax was repealed by Quebec in 1986.

- After the new Canadian citizen's five-year tax free residency, a Canadian who moves his or her residence to another country is taxed by Revenue Canada (their Internal Revenue Service) only on income earned or paid from within Canada - not on the person's worldwide income, a distinct tax advantage Americans living abroad do not enjoy.

However, a naturalized Canadian citizen who lives ten consecutive years or more outside Canada can be stripped of citizenship at the discretion of the government, a point to keep in mind when planning your future.

Consider This Scenario

Let's suppose a wealthy American citizen planning for the future wishes to sell an established business, or for that matter, convert fixed assets into liquid cash for investment or other purposes. Depending on how long the property has been held and how the liquidation deal is structured, the seller may face U.S. capital gains taxes at the current maximum rate of 38 percent.

Depending on the seller's tax bracket, increased income taxes can be 40 percent or more. In either case, a major part of the cash proceeds from the sale or conversion will be devoured by the U.S. Internal Revenue Service and state tax authorities before the seller ever sees a thin dime.

How can this enormous tax burden be avoided?

What if title to the U.S. business or assets is transferred to a foreign trust (with the property owner as the beneficiary) or to a corporation he or she controls, conveniently located in a low or no-tax offshore jurisdiction?

And what if, after the trust or corporation receives title, the former U.S. owner/donor applies for and receives Canadian citizenship, renounces U.S. citizenship and becomes a legal resident of Canada for at least five years?

That offshore trust or corporation will have a five-year period in which to pay benefits or income to the ex-U.S./new Canadian citizen - a free spirit who will have absolutely no income or capital gains tax liability in either the U.S. or Canada - _if_ that intrepid person carefully follows every step required by the U.S. and Canadian laws that are available to accomplish this unique tax-free status.

It sounds to good to be true? Read on.

Becoming a Canadian

Interested Americans

For anyone interested in obtaining Canadian citizenship it is advisable to explore fully any possible family ties one may have to the country. The Canadian

Using Canada as a Stepping Stone

government is helpful in providing answers about whether a foreign national may be eligible by law for Canadian citizenship based on ancestry. Any Canadian consulate will provide a personal history information form to be completed and submitted with copies of relevant birth records to the Registrar of Canadian Citizenship in the capital city of Ottawa.

A "Certificate of Canadian Citizenship" is automatically issued to anyone who qualifies for citizenship by family descent, and this can serve as the least complicated basis on which to establish a new legal residence in Canada.

Maybe you would like to test personally the northern waters before making any major decision about a future in Canada. Fortunately, Americans thinking about immigrating can explore life north of the border for an extended period. Since 1989 the U.S.-Canadian Free Trade Agreement has allowed reciprocal extended stays of up to one year, with no requirement to obtain a special visa. Americans employed in certain occupations can enter, live and work in Canada without a permit and with no prior approval, and the number of one-year extensions is unlimited.

This right to work in Canada includes those Americans working for U.S. firms who do research and designing, purchasing, sales and contract negotiation, customs brokering, financial services, public relations, advertising, tourism and market research. It also includes professionals, so long as they are paid by a U.S. source.

As a general rule, Canada and the United States have the longest open border of any two neighboring nations in the world. Entry to either country requires no special visa or passport, only proper personal identification such as a state or provincial motor vehicle operators license or voters card. Tourists automatically are allowed to stay for at least 90 days without special permission.

One thing is certain - Americans and Canadians are no strangers to each other. U.S. investors own over 50 percent of all Canadian manufacturing and are the fourth largest investors in the total economy, after investors from Great

Britain, the Netherlands and Japan. Overall, the U.S. has $73 billion invested in Canada and Canadians hold $51.2 billion in U.S. assets. The two nations have the largest bi-lateral volume of annual trade in the world; in 1994 it encompassed $100.4 billion in exports from the U.S., and $11.2 billion in Canadian exports to America.

Open Door for Immigrant Investors

Though there certainly is concern among Canadians about increased immigration, Canada keeps the official welcome mat out for skilled workers, professionals - and especially *for wealthy investors who wish to become Canadian citizens.*

Independent applicants for "permanent residence" - as Canadians call immigrant status - are rated on a point system that takes into account age, education, fluency in English and French, financial standing, occupational or professional experience, training and local demand for certain types of workers, geographic destination and a personal assessment of the applicant. Certain needed occupations are favored. Seventy points and up is passing.

The common method for prospective new immigrants is to obtain work from a Canadian employer in advance of an application for entry, or by applying for an immigrant visa with a job offer already in hand.

Completely separate from the point system for admissions, Canadian law favors as a special "independent class" certain preferred immigrants including investors, entrepreneurs, the self-employed and those who will add to the "cultural and artistic life" of the nation. With minor variation in the each of the provinces, investor-immigrants generally must have a net worth in excess of C$500,000 and be willing to invest at least C$250,000 in Canada for a minimum three-to-five year period.

With proof of sufficient assets and an attractive business plan, especially one creating new jobs for Canadians, an investor applicant's "permanent residence" and eventual citizenship is almost assured. Government loan guarantees and other assistance may be available for investors willing to invest larger sums of C $750,000 or more. This investor visa category has been heavily used by wealthy Hong Kong Chinese moving to Vancouver, now home to a large and influential Asian-Canadian community.

For potential investor visa applicants, the government rolls out the proverbial "red carpet," officially known as the "Business Migration Programme." Business experience, marketing skills, contacts within Canada and an adequate credit rating and available funds all greatly increase this type of applicant's chance of success.

Applicants are usually required to submit detailed business proposals or general business plans, which must accompany the application for permanent residence. Such plans must detail the nature of the business, operating procedures, key personnel (which may just be the applicant), marketing and a financial plan. As in the U.S., the usual forms for business in Canada include the sole proprietorship, general and limited partnerships and corporations.

Canadian Immigration Process

There you receive an "Immigration Questionnaire" requiring basic personal information about you, your spouse and family. Once this is submitted and checked, within a few weeks a more detailed questionnaire will be presented if the applicant is found initially acceptable. After this second document is reviewed, a personal interview is required and then, medical examinations for the applicant, spouse and family will be needed.

If all goes well, shortly thereafter you will receive a visa for entry into Canada as a landed immigrant: "Welcome, bien venue a Canada."

It is worth noting that Canada recognizes the principle of dual nationality, allowing successful applicants for citizenship to retain their nationality of origin. For reasons that will become obvious in a moment, that choice is not a viable option for an ex-American becoming a Canadian citizen in order to obtain the five-year tax relief the law offers.

Another advantage that comes with this new citizenship is the international official acceptance of the Canadian passport, one of the most respected in the world.

The Big Change - U.S. Expatriation

Later we'll describe more fully the amazing potential tax savings that await you north of the border, but first let's face the hard realities essential to make this tax free plan work for a willing new Canadian immigrant.

The potential immigrant from America will have to give up United States citizenship, formally renouncing his or her U.S. status in a way that carefully avoids identifying the purpose as avoidance of U.S. taxes - otherwise the IRS will pursue you and any U.S. income or assets you may have. (For the record, fewer than a thousand Americans renounce their citizenship each year).

Goodbye to the IRS

Under current U.S. law (section 877 of the Foreign Investors Tax Act of 1966) a citizen who is suspected of giving up U.S. citizenship for "the principal purpose" of avoiding taxes can still be taxed on U.S. source income for up to ten years after leaving the country, and if he or she dies in that period, the IRS can go after the assets in the estate still located in the U.S. or any payments made to U.S. beneficiaries and heirs of the decedent's estate.

However, don't get too nervous. The truth is - this law leaks like a sieve because American expatriates, long before renouncing U.S. citizenship, routinely restructure their assets, sending wealth abroad to avoid the grasp of the IRS. The U.S. Treasury openly admits monitoring of such subjective private transactions is all but impossible. And this difficulty of proof of intentions is why the recent debate in Congress about a proposed "expatriation tax" on unrealized capital gains is so much political hot air. By the time someone at IRS figures out an expatriation tax might be due, the person is long gone from the United States - along with his or her liquid assets and wealth.

Do It the Right Way

Here's how expatriation from the U.S. can be accomplished, while avoiding pitfalls along the way:

It is crucial to obtain proper legal advice on expatriation in order to be effective in renouncing citizenship. The worst case is to wind up in an ambiguous dual national status with U.S. citizenship retained and a new citizenship added - you then may find yourself within the potential grasp of two government taxing authorities.

Generally, an ex-American who properly renounces citizenship is treated by U.S. law as a non-resident alien, taxable at a flat 30 percent rate only on certain types of passive income derived from U.S. sources, and on net profits of the sale of a U.S. trade or business at regular graduated rates. Such a person can usually safely spend only about 122 days a year within the United States, before exposing themselves to IRS claims for full U.S. taxation based on alien residency risked by a longer stay.

Remember, the U.S. is one of the few countries that imposes income and estate taxes on its citizens on their worldwide income and assets, regardless of where the person is a resident or where those assets are located. That's exactly why Canadian citizenship can be so valuable to an ex-American - Revenue Canada doesn't tax worldwide income of citizens living abroad like the IRS does for Americans.

Another strict caution: you must be certain to obtain valid Canadian citizenship before you renounce your U.S. citizenship - so that you do not find yourself a "stateless" person, "the man without a country." A person without a passport and a nationality is legally lost in this world of national borders and

Residence Havens

customs officials - and as such is not entitled to the legal protection of any government.

The Wall Street Journal reported in 1995 that one poor soul has been living on a bench in the international waiting area of DeGaulle Airport near Paris for the past two years, while several governments and the U.N. Refugee Commission fight over his nationality!

With no valid passport, international travel is difficult if not impossible, and a person who renounces U.S. nationality must apply for a visa to return to the U.S., just as any other alien does. If found ineligible for a visa, the ex-U.S. citizen can be barred from entering the United States.

Your Right to Leave

Every American has the unconditional power to relinquish his or her United States citizenship. Section 349(a) of the Immigration and Nationality Act (8 U.S.C. 1481) states:

A person who is a national of the United States whether by birth or naturalization, shall lose his nationality by voluntarily performing any of the following acts with the intention of relinquishing United States nationality:

(four paragraphs of involuntary acts omitted)

(5) making a formal renunciation of nationality before a diplomatic or consular officer of the United States in a foreign state, in such form as may be prescribed by the Secretary of State . . .

Valid renunciation must be an unequivocal act in which a person manifests an unqualified intention to relinquish U.S. citizenship. In order for renunciation to be effective, all of the conditions of the statute must be met; the person must appear in person and sign an oath of renunciation before a U.S. consular or diplomatic officer, usually at an American Embassy or Consulate. Renunciations not in the form prescribed by the U.S. Secretary of State have no legal effect.

Using Canada as a Stepping Stone

Because of the way in which Section 349(a)(5) is written and interpreted, Americans cannot effectively renounce their citizenship by mail, through an agent, or while within the United States.

Once a renunciation is accomplished before an American diplomatic or consular officer abroad, all documents are referred to the U.S. Department of State. The Office of Overseas Citizens Services reviews them to ensure that all criteria under the law are met, but the State Department has no discretion to refuse a proper renunciation - the personal right to renounce is absolute.

Long before such a drastic final step is taken towards ending U.S. citizenship, the new Canadian immigrant should have his or her official Canadian citizenship in order, papers in hand and an established residence in their new homeland - most likely in Montreal, Toronto or Vancouver where the vast majority of immigrants decide to live.

Essential Preliminaries

The Immigrant Offshore Trust

The key to eligibility for this unusual, Canadian tax-free "window of opportunity" for wealthy Americans willing to surrender U.S. citizenship and become Canadian citizens is found in section 94(1) of Canada's Income Tax Act of 1952 ("the Act").

In essence, section 94 ensures that an immigrant who has never been a Canadian resident can live in Canada and earn tax-free foreign source income from a non-resident trust or affiliated corporation, for the first five calendar years of the immigrant's Canadian residency.

For planning purposes, Canadian residency should begin not in January, but in December of the first year of residency, so that the person will benefit from five full calendar years - 60 months - of tax freedom. The law grants this privilege for all or part of the first five calendar years of residency, not for five years from the first date of residency.

The Beneficiary

To qualify for this big tax break, the arrangement must include:

a) an immigrant person resident in Canada, and either

b) a foreign corporation or a trust (wherever located) with which the person in Canada is "closely tied" (meaning, according to court decisions, "not dealing at arm's length"), or

c) a foreign affiliate corporation controlled by a person resident in Canada, as defined by law (about which we will have more to say later).

The essential factor is that the non-resident trust must have one or more beneficiaries who are Canadian residents, or the offshore corporation must be "closely tied" in some manner to one or more Canadian residents.

The beneficiaries likely will be your family members, and can include yourself. The foreign trustee will follow your instructions on how the trust assets should be invested and income disbursed. Except for the distance involved, you will notice very little difference in your financial operations.

Under Canada's revenue laws (subsection 248(25) of the Act) a "beneficial interest" in a non-resident trust is defined as belonging to a person or partnership that holds any right - immediate or future, absolute or contingent, conditional or otherwise - to receive any of the income or principal capital of the trust, either directly or indirectly.

It would be difficult to find a broader definition of "beneficial entitlement" than this - and the implications for tax avoidance are obvious and potentially enormous.

What's more, Canadian tax officials and court cases have repeatedly stated that such "immigration trusts" and related businesses, when properly created and managed abroad, are not an abuse of the tax laws, because section

94 clearly is designed as a vehicle for exempting new immigrants from taxation for the stated period of five years. In the case of almost every other tax-avoidance scheme, Revenue Canada would pounce. Here the law does more than permit tax avoidance, it approves and encourages it.

Only a change in Canadian law by Parliament could remove this generous tax break, and there is no current talk of removing a provision that has been so successful in attracting needed capital and business to the nation.

Trust Property Sources

In order for a non-resident trust or a non-resident corporation that qualifies as a "controlled foreign affiliate" to receive section 94 tax-free treatment, it must have acquired its property (which, note carefully, can include guaranteeing or making a loan to the trust or company) from a particular person who meets all of the following requirements:

a) the donor must be the trust or affiliate corporation beneficiary, or related to the beneficiary (spouse, child, parent), or be the uncle, aunt, nephew or niece of the beneficiary;

b) the donor must have been resident in Canada at any time in an 18-month period before the end of the trust's first taxation year or before his or her death;

c) if the trust property came from an individual, the individual donor eventually must be a resident in Canada for a period or periods totalling more than sixty months.

Section 94 applies regardless of the method by which the non-resident trust or corporation acquires its property including purchase, gift, bequest, inheritance or exercise of a power of appointment by or from an individual. The law treats all such transfers as if the donor had transferred his or her property to the trust or corporation.

There are some restrictions on the donor to an offshore trust that must be carefully avoided. The donor cannot retain any reversion right or power to designate beneficiaries after the trust is created - this is what is known as an irrevocable living trust. He or she cannot retain any control over how the trust property will be disposed of during the donor's lifetime. If the property is donated to an offshore corporation, the donor cannot retain any greater interest in the company than a 10 percent equity ownership.

As a general rule a trust donor should transfer only cash and title to intangible assets (stocks, bonds, etc.) to an offshore trust. Portable assets, such as gold coins or diamonds, also can be used.

Title to real estate or a business located in Canada or the United States definitely should not be made a part of the trust property. Transfer of tangible property physically located in either nation does nothing to keep those assets away from Canadian or American creditors or tax authorities, and could subject the trust to the jurisdiction of a Canadian court. By holding title to assets within Canada, the offshore trust could be deemed to be doing business in Canada and therefore liable for Canadian taxes.

Foreign Control A Must

In order to determine if an offshore trust is "non-resident" from a tax perspective, Revenue Canada looks to the incidents of control and ownership.

The residence of a trust by ascertaining where the managing trustees or the persons who control the trust assets actually reside. It is therefore important that the offshore trust have a majority of trustees living in the foreign jurisdiction where the trust is registered and where its operation is located.

This requirement for majority offshore control does not diminish the ability of a trust beneficiary to serve as a trustee, and to live in Canada. Neither status jeopardizes the offshore, and therefore tax-free, status of the trust.

Canadian tax law specifically allows offshore immigration trusts to receive tax-free income from investment business conducted by a Canadian citizen living in Canada during the five-year residency period required under section 94.

Thus the new Canadian investor-citizen is free to roam the world by phone, fax, telex, wire, courier or letter, using his capital and ability to produce profits for the trust and its beneficiaries. But to maximize tax avoidance, the trust should not carry on other active business in Canada or invest in property located in Canada, sale of, or income from which otherwise may subject the trust to certain domestic taxes because of the Canadian source or location.

Creating an Offshore Immigration Trust

When creation of an offshore trust is considered, whether for Canadian tax purposes under section 94, for general asset protection, or to shift and shield income from high taxes in the trust donor's country of residence (wherever that may be), a tax haven country is the natural location for sensible trust creation and operation.

With a goal of paying no taxes and/or avoiding taxes at home, one must look abroad for a friendly national jurisdiction in which to locate, a place where little or no taxes are imposed - and where a section 94-qualified enterprise will be legitimate and welcome.

Although it wasn't always so, today a foreign trust located in a tax haven nation is an internationally established and proven fixture in effective offshore financial planning. This type of trust is the safety vehicle that places personal assets beyond the reach of many irritants: your native taxing authorities, potential litigation plaintiffs, an irate spouse or unreasonable creditors, where ever such opponents may be located.

Even though an offshore immigration trust can guarantee five tax-free years for the new Canadian citizen, some of the most important advantages are the non-tax benefits. To other Canadian citizens ineligible for section 94 status, the asset protection benefits of an offshore trust can be far more valuable than potential tax savings, although those are also available. Having such a trust allows Canadians not only the protection of their assets from creditors, but a high degree of financial privacy, flexible estate planning and the ability to engage in international and diversified investments unrestricted by domestic Canadian law.

Many wealthy Canadians today have at least one financial foe they fear more than Revenue Canada - an irate plaintiff's lawyer. As in the U.S., business and professional people too often suffer at the hands of a legal system with judges eager and willing to give others peoples' assets to a sympathy-inspiring plaintiff. One mistake, one unfortunate accident, can take away the fruits of life's labors, and insurance companies often cannot or will not cover fully liability claims. The offshore trust can do the protective job when others won't.

Because of this, many successful professionals and business owners are putting a higher priority on asset preservation than on tax avoidance. A foreign offshore trust is an excellent means to preserve one's wealth, a point to remember as the five-year Canadian tax moratorium nears its end.

A Word About Tax Havens

Simply stated, a tax haven is any country whose laws, regulations, traditions, and usually, international treaty arrangements make it possible for any person, trust or corporation, domestic or foreign, to reduce their overall tax burden. This can be accomplished by moving existing operations into the tax haven jurisdiction or by establishing a new legal entity within the country. This general definition, however, covers many types of tax havens, and it is important to understand the differences.

"No Tax" Havens

These are countries with no personal or corporate income, capital gains, or wealth taxes, places where you can easily incorporate a business and/or form a trust. The governments of these countries do earn some revenue from corporations and trusts, imposing small fees on documents of incorporation, a charge on the value of corporate shares and annual registration fees.

Primary examples of such countries are the British Crown Colonies of Bermuda and the Cayman Islands, and the Commonwealth of the Bahamas, an independent nation within the British Commonwealth of Nations.

Consider for example, the Cayman Islands tax structure.

There are no taxes levied except stamp taxes on certain transactions and import duties. Non-residents who form exempted corporations automatically qualify for and receive a government guarantee of no taxes for twenty years; trusts are given a fifty year no-tax guarantee.

The process of incorporation is quick, easy, simple and cheap. It can be done in a matter of hours at the office of the Registrar of Companies in George Town, the capital city located on Grand Cayman Island, only 475 air miles from Miami International Airport.

There is a registration fee and an annual operating fee thereafter. Start up costs will run about $2,500, with a yearly operating cost of about $1,500. Establishing a trust can cost about $1,000. The Caymans corporation and trusts statutes allow a wide range of business activities, stock issues and great flexibility in actual operation.

The Caymans are noted for laws strongly protecting corporate and bank privacy with stiff penalties of fines and prison for any one, including government officials, who violates the law.

Unlike a corporate charter and bylaws, the actual language of a trust agreement is not registered with government authorities in most countries.

251

Some tax haven countries require registering trusts agreements, so you must consider whether this is helpful or harmful from your point of view. In most cases the terms of the agreement are between you and the trustee, unless a dispute forces one of you to bring the trust agreement into court. Many trust beneficiaries have never seen the trust agreements.

Here's how a Canadian can establish a financial base in the Caymans (or some other tax haven):

Let's say you have $3 million you wish to invest, but being a reasonable person, you want to avoid Canadian taxes on the income produced from your investment. The new immigrant has five years of tax freedom, but other Canadians can also use the Caymans to cut taxes.

First you need a non-resident of Canada - a friend or relative to act as manager of your offshore investment corporation which will be registered in George Town - you can't do it yourself, since the new Canadian immigrant must live in Canada for five years. You transfer the $3 million to an offshore Cayman-registered trust, also administered by your friend as trustee, probably in the same George Town office. That money is invested by the trust in Canadian government treasury bills or public company stocks, and the interest income this produces can be paid by the trust to you, your children or other named beneficiaries tax free. At current interest rates that means a savings of about $100,000 a year in taxes.

While this tax haven structure - a Cayman corporation and a trust - may seem expensive to establish, the arrangement qualifies under section 94 for five-years of tax free income for trust beneficiaries. After the five year period ends, this arrangement can continue to shield the Canadian beneficiary from taxes, so long as it is controlled by non-Canadians.

The worst that can happen if Revenue Canada challenges the post-five year operation, is taxation imposed at the rate you would have suffered had you not tried to continue offshore - plus non-deductible interest on the reassessed taxes and a few thousands of dollars in cost for the legal paperwork and registration in the no-tax Caymans. The best possible result will be major tax savings you could obtain in no other way.

"No Tax on Foreign Income" Havens

Countries in this category impose income taxes, both on individuals and corporations, but only on income earned within that country, not abroad. The laws here exempt from tax any income earned from foreign sources involving no local business activities, apart from simple "housekeeping" matters. For example, there is often no tax on income derived from the export of local manufactured goods, since these countries wish to encourage domestic industrial expansion and local jobs.

The "no-tax-on-foreign-income havens" break down into two groups. There are those; 1) that allow a corporation to do business both internally and externally, taxing only the income coming from internal domestic sources; and, 2) those requiring a company to choose at the time of incorporation whether it will do business locally, with consequent tax liabilities, or will do only foreign business, and thus be exempt from taxation.

Primary examples in these two categories are the Republic of Panama, the British colony of Gibraltar and the United Kingdom-associated islands of Jersey, Guernsey, the Isle of Man.

"Low Tax" Havens

Countries in this status impose some taxes on all corporate income, wherever earned worldwide. However, most have international double-taxation agreements with high-tax countries like Canada, that may reduce the withholding tax imposed on income earned in the high-tax countries by the local corporations. Cyprus is a primary example. Barbados is another

Residence Havens

low-tax country (with a 2.5 percent tax on corporate income) popular with Canadian business people, about which more below.

"Special" Tax Havens

These countries impose all or most of the usual taxes, but either allow valuable tax concessions, write-offs or "holidays" to special types of companies they wish to encourage (such as a total tax exemption for shipping companies, movie production companies, or financial and investment institutions), or they allow special types of corporate organization, such as the highly flexible corporate arrangements offered by the Grand Duchy of Liechtenstein.

The Netherlands and Ireland are particularly good examples of nations which offer major tax concessions to selected foreign businesses.

Ireland - Special Opportunities

Just as with Barbados, the Republic of Ireland can also be used as the location of an offshore corporate affiliate - giving you commercial access to 340 million potential customers who live within the boundaries of the European Community.

Using Ireland as an affiliate base is one way to lock in low labor costs and a 20-year tax holiday in the process. In some cases, you can even get free government money to fund your start-up costs. Irish labor costs are only 60% to 70% of Canadian wage levels, there is a 10% ceiling on corporate taxes, and cash grants are available to lure foreign business investors.

Since the 1970s, the Irish government has pursued an aggressive foreign investment program. To encourage foreign entrepreneurs to set up businesses, the government created the Irish Development Authority (IDA). To qualify for IDA incentives, a company must be engaged either in manufacturing or in international services. The latter category includes computer or software services, offices for insurance companies, and financial and other primary services.

The Irish parliament has passed a law extending through the year 2010 the maximum corporate tax rate of 10% on foreign investments. Thus, Canadian companies investing now can look forward to fifteen years of substantial tax relief. The government cash grants can take the form either of picking up the entire first year's payroll for a labor intensive business, such as software development, or of capital grants for factories or other more capital-intensive operations.

In addition to the IDA program, Ireland offers other programs. One of them is the Shannon Free Zone program. Incentives are similar to those of the IDA, with taxes held to 10% and capital grants available. Companies are required to locate near Shannon Airport. The Shannon Free Zone operation is administered separately from the IDA.

Ireland offers many advantages compared with rival centers such as Luxembourg and the Channel Islands, through lower wage and housing costs, a skilled and abundant labor force and good communications with other European business centers.

One of the IFSC's attractions has been the possibility for cash-rich firms to place their surplus cash in investment funds which are then managed in Dublin by specialist companies. Profits are taxed at the 10 per cent rate and can be repatriated without further tax liabilities due to Ireland's double taxation treaties with its EU partners.

A Need for Caution

The objective of an offshore tax haven is the legal reduction of your tax obligations.

Keep in mind it will do you no good to suffer the bother of restructuring your financial life, only to find yourself embroiled in years of complex and

Residence Havens

expensive court battles with Revenue Canada. Or worse, finding yourself facing criminal charges for tax evasion, or a variety of other possible tax crimes.

Reasonable caution places a premium on pursuing the correct path from the very beginning in order to qualify for initial section 94 tax-free treatment, and this means the assistance of competent, expert advice from the very start. Cutting corners can only mean you and your financial advisors could be in deep trouble.

The Mechanics of Offshore Business

An Ideal Offshore Location

The country in which your Canadian immigration trust and the managing trustee are located should be, for obvious reasons, a nation with strong financial privacy laws. Most tax haven countries do emphasize such statutory privacy rights.

The ideal places for establishing asset-preservation or tax avoidance trusts are tax haven countries such as Nevis, the Cayman Islands, Jersey, the Channel Islands, and the Cook Islands in the south Pacific, among others. These countries have statutory law tailored to your financial needs.

Trustees are not required to divulge information about assets held by a trust - and cannot be forced by Canadian courts to turn over trust assets to Revenue Canada or other Canadian creditors - unless and until those creditors go through the host country's judicial system at great expense and with a lot of time-consuming effort.

Creation of an offshore immigration or other trust will affect your personal tax return only in that a taxpayer must disclose the existence of an offshore trust on his or her annual federal tax return.

From the wealth protection aspect, creditors must get a court to order you to reveal your tax return and the existence of the trust, and that takes time. If they do discover the trust's offshore location and file a collection suit in the haven country, local laws are hostile to non-resident creditors and the trustee can shift the trust and its assets to another country and another trustee in an emergency. Then pursuing creditors must begin the process all over again.

Many of these foreign jurisdictions do not recognize U.S., Canadian or any non-domestic court orders, and a creditor must retry completely the original claim which gave rise to a Canadian or U.S. court judgment. Under such circumstances, it won't be long before the creditor will want to talk about settling the dispute.

The Trust Advantage

This gives trusts a distinct privacy advantage over corporations.

In every tax haven country at least one person involved in organizing a corporation must be listed on the public record, along with the name and address of the corporation. In most countries the directors must be listed on the original charter, but in a few maximum privacy countries only the organizing lawyer is listed, but even that reference gives privacy invaders a starting point from which to work against you.

With a trust, in most offshore havens, nothing other than its existence is required to be registered - and often not even that fact. The trust agreement and the parties involved do not have to be disclosed, and there is little or nothing on the public record. In privacy-conscious countries, the trustee is allowed to reveal information about the trust only in very limited circumstances.

The country chosen for such a trust must have local trust experts who understand fully and can assist you in your objectives. The foreign local attorney who creates your trust unquestionably must know the applicable law and tax consequences.

Once established, the offshore immigration trust in its basic form can consist of as little as a trust account in an international bank located in the foreign country. Many well established multi-national Canadian banks can provide trustees for such arrangements and are experienced in such matters - but, as an extra level of insulation from government pressure, you might want to consider using a non-Canadian bank.

With today's instant communications and international banking facilities it is as convenient to hold assets and accounts overseas as it is in another Canadian or U.S. city. Most international banks offer Canadian and U.S. dollar-denominated accounts which often have better interest rates than Canadian institutions.

Trust Creation Advantages

Depending on the country of choice, the settlor of an offshore trust can gain many advantages including the exercise of far greater control over assets and income from the trust than permitted under domestic Canadian law.

The trust can provide privacy, confidentiality, and reduced domestic reporting requirements in Canada; avoidance of domestic taxes and probate in case death taxes are reimposed; increased flexibility in conducting affairs in case of disability, in transferring assets, international investing, or avoiding possible domestic currency controls. A foreign trust can also substitute for or supplement costly professional liability insurance or even a prenuptial agreement as protection for your heirs and their inheritance.

Trust Structure

The structure of an offshore immigration trust is not very different from that of a domestic Canadian trust.

The settlor creates the trust by transferring title to his assets to the trust, to be administered by a trustee according to the terms of the trust declaration.

Usually the trustee is a bank in the offshore jurisdiction chosen. Beneficiaries can vary according to the settlor's estate planning objectives and the settlor himself, may be a beneficiary under section 94.

Many foreign jurisdictions also permit appointment of a trust "protector" who, as the title indicates, oversees the operation of the trust to insure its objectives are being met and the local law is followed. A protector does not manage the trust, but can veto actions in limited instances.

The greatest worry about a foreign asset protection trust often is the distance between you, your assets and the people who manage them. While your assets do not have to be transferred physically to the foreign country in which the trust exists, circumstances may dictate such a precautionary transfer. Without such a physical transfer, a Canadian court could decide to disregard the trust and take possession of the assets.

When considering a foreign country in which to located your trust you should find out whether local laws are favorable, clear, and offer the certain protection you seek. Check the past economic and political stability of the country, the reputation of its judicial system, local tax laws, the business climate, language barriers and available communication and financial facilities.

Several offshore financial centers have developed legislation hospitable to foreign-owned asset protection trusts, among them the Caribbean-area nations of Nevis, the Cayman Islands, the Bahamas, Belize, the Turks and Caicos Islands, and the Cook Islands near New Zealand, as well as Cyprus and Gibraltar in the Mediterranean.

Most of these countries have laws preventing foreign creditors from attacking trust assets unless the suit is brought within two years from the date of the trust creation.

Residence Havens

The Offshore Corporation

The offshore corporation is best suited for the needs of Canadian business owners who wish to do good business - and also do very well for themselves when it comes to lowering their taxes and increasing profits. Under section 94, "affiliated" offshore corporations qualify as sources of income for the new immigrant granted five-year tax freedom - and the company can be used for tax-avoidance after the five-year moratorium ends, as we explain below.

But foreign corporations, as Revenue Canada demands, must be more than a mere "sham." A full-scale company, complete with working offices, staff, international fax and telecommunications facilities, bank accounts, a registered agent, board of directors, a local attorney and an accountant can cost upwards of $50,000 annually.

Members of your board of directors, associates of the local tax specialists who help you form the company, will be paid about $2,500 a year. There will be annual taxes to pay and reports to be filed with the local government, and with Canada.

As the Canadian owner you will want to visit your company offices once or twice a year, a pleasant enough activity if you locate your business in one of the tropical venues specializing in such corporate arrangements - the Bahamas or the Cayman Islands, for example. January is an excellent month to visit.

How It Works

Let's say as a new investor immigrant you purchase a Canadian manufacturing business exporting $5 million in products around the world each year.

Because you are a legitimate business with established foreign transactions, your Canadian company can incorporate an offshore affiliate in say, Barbados - like Canada, a member of the British Commonwealth, and a place where international companies pay only 2.5 percent corporate income tax - unlike Canada's 45 percent.

There are less than three quarters of a million people living on this pleasant, tropical 166-square-mile island, where the mean temperature hovers between 76 and 80 degrees fahrenheit all year round.

You can set up your affiliate with offices in the capital, Bridgetown (population 8,000), a city with eight major international banks, including branches of the Royal Bank of Canada and the Canadian Imperial Bank of Commerce - as well as Chase Manhattan and Barclays. Regular air service is offered by Air Canada, British Airways and American, among others.

Your Bridgetown affiliate will handle all foreign sales and international marketing for your Canadian company, for its services charging a 15 percent mark-up on the value of the goods it sells, or about $750,000 a year, at your current export levels.

What you have done is legally transfer your Canada profits to your offshore affiliate where taxes are much lower - 2.5 percent vs. 45 percent! After gladly paying $18,750 in Barbados local corporate income taxes, the rest of the money, $731,250, can be sent back to Canada as a dividend from exempt surplus income, paid to the parent company - tax free! And during the first five years of your citizenship, you personally can share in that corporate income tax free!

Even after your five years of tax grace ends, until the parent company shareholders need the money for their own use, or until they sell the business, Canadian taxes on the income can be deferred indefinitely. If the shareholders want payment immediately, it can be paid out as dividends - and taxed by Canada at the rate of 36 percent, well below the personal income tax rate of 50 percent plus.

Investment Potential

The Barbados affiliate could also serve as an investment arm for your parent company, actively making international investments. All the earned income from such investments - dividends, interest and capital gains - will go to your Bridgetown affiliate, and be taxed at the 2.5 percent rate. Investment profits can also be sent to the parent company, tax free. In order to follow this course successfully, meeting the rule requirements laid own by Revenue Canada, all corporate investment decisions must originate with your Bridgetown money manager, who runs your affiliate on a daily basis - it cannot be you dictating every move by phone from Montreal or Ottawa.

As an added consideration, those with experience say that in order to be successful in using foreign affiliates for investment purposes, a minimum of $1 million in initial capital is needed to start.

In theory this all sounds grand, but there are practical problems associated with an offshore corporation.

First of all, just as in establishing a domestic corporation, legal formalities must be strictly observed when you incorporate abroad - Revenue Canada will check this carefully - and, as we said, the cost of starting up can be considerable. You will need a local legal counsel who knows the law and understands your business and tax objectives. Corporations anywhere are rule-bound creatures requiring separate books and records, meetings, minutes and corporate authorizing resolutions which make it less flexible than many other arrangements.

But you can pay for a whole lot of record keeping with the money you can save.

Reliable Sources of Help

In setting up an offshore trust, it is important to consult with an advisor who understands the benefits, limitations, and intricacies inherent in such ventures. A number of well-qualified advisors are suggested in the investing chapter.

Once you have a trust, for assets other than your Canadian business, it is advisable to have offshore management of the passive investments. For asset management and securities brokerage, recommendations will also be found in the investing chapter.

Afterward

When Five Years End

When the five year residency requirement of the new Canadian citizen nears its end, the offshore trust can either be converted to a domestic Canadian trust (by passing majority control to trustees who reside in Canada), or its affairs can be terminated and the assets distributed to the beneficiaries, in which case they will owe Canadian capital gains taxes on the fair market value at the time of distribution.

That's not a very attractive prospect because the 1995 federal budget eliminated the previous $100,000 capital gains tax exemption.

Once an offshore trust is converted into a domestic trust, its income will be taxed at a rate that varies in each province, but, as we have noted, generally is in the brutal range of 45 to 55 percent.

As for income taxes, Canadians earning US $43,000 and up are taxed on individual income at the top rate ranging over 50 percent, and, as we have pointed out, the tax on corporation income is now as high as 45 percent. The highest effective combined federal-provincial personal income tax rate in 1994 was in the province of Ontario at 52.35 percent.

All of which means you might well plan for residency elsewhere after your five-year, tax-free moratorium expires. We repeat, Canada has no estate taxes and does not levy income taxes on its citizens who live abroad, except on income earned in Canada or assets located within Canada.

Foreign Attractions

After five years of no taxes it won't be easy to face the music of Revenue Canada, especially comparing the outrageously high Canadian income taxes with those imposed in tax haven foreign countries - where, as we have seen, rates for income and corporate taxes are in the low single digits. Prudent Canadians, even if they are not new immigrants, can take advantage of this wide international tax disparity by establishing an offshore tax shelter that can easily double after tax disposable income.

This can be accomplished in full compliance with federal law and the tax code - so that Revenue Canada cannot mount a successful challenge, though based on recent history, RC may well go after anything they consider "overly aggressive tax strategies."

Aggressive Tax Enforcement

The most dangerous attitude one can adopt when dealing with the establishment of offshore business arrangements is the cavalier approach - the idea that "white collar" crimes are somehow less serious than violent crimes, like bank robbery; or the notion that the federal government is less concerned about tax or financial offenses than they are about other civil wrongs.

And don't think geographic distance offers any sure protection for those who want to bend the law by going offshore. During the last fifteen years, Canada has rapidly expanded its tax treaty relations - bilateral and multilateral

- aimed at both tax avoidance and tax evasion. Canada now has more than sixty mutual tax agreements in force, or under negotiation with foreign governments.

Canadian courts display a stiff attitude towards tax scofflaws, and the judicial long arm reaches across oceans. For example, the Canadian Supreme Court in Robert Spencer v. R, 85 DTC 5446, held that the former manager of the Freeport branch of the Canadian Royal Bank could be forced to give testimony at a tax evasion trial in Canada, even though doing so would be a breach of the Bahamian bank secrecy law.

The federal government and Revenue Canada's vigorous international tax enforcement efforts have been aided by new and powerful laws aimed at tax avoidance practices. Laws were changed to extend the statute of limitations on government questioning of certain offshore tax transactions from three to six years; RC was given greatly increased powers to obtain "foreign-based information or documents" about a Canadian citizen's business activities abroad; and elaborate, detailed annual corporate reporting requirements were imposed on "intercompany transactions" between Canadians and any offshore affiliated entities. Failure to report or false statements concerning such transactions can cause fines of up to $24,000.

Revenue Canada keeps an eagle eye on the tax shelter industry, and tracks the offshore business activity of individual Canadians, as best it can. Whether RC employing its own informational sources finds out about offshore activity or not, reporting requirements concerning foreign investments squarely place personal responsibility on taxpayers to reveal what they are doing abroad - or suffer the legal consequences if they get caught for not reporting.

In spite of these tough federal tax enforcement policies and an array of laws with sharp teeth, there are still many lawful opportunities for offshore financial activities designed to minimize the impact of Canada's high tax rates. Offshore tax havens are legal, and in selective circumstances there are useful

Residence Havens

ways in which non-resident owned international investment and business structures can serve you by reducing substantially your exposure to the high taxes of Canada.

Tax Shelters Under Siege

With the exception of the section 94 immigrant trust, Parliament in recent years has "cracked down" on tax shelters, particularly those operating domestically, and this approach includes the 1988 adoption of the infamous "General Anti-Avoidance Rule"or "GAAR," for short.

This radical rule gives Revenue Canada the discretionary retroactive power to revisit and recharacterize for increased taxation purposes, any business transaction which RC interprets as having no "bona fide purpose" - other than to effect a tax savings.

This places squarely on business the burden of demonstrating a "bona fide purpose," (other than tax saving) in order to obtain that savings - and as you might imagine, there have been more than a few court cases contesting the rule's application, scope and still unsettled meaning. That this Draconian rule even exists should give you an accurate idea of the essence - and the direction of federal tax policy.

Before you get nervous, you should know Revenue Canada has ruled that the GAAR specifically does not apply to the tax-free, five-year immigration trusts authorized under section 94.

Strangely enough, the anti-tax shelter government attitude generally does not extend to other offshore tax entities, still governed for the most part by the "Foreign Affiliate System" statute of 1972. This law allows plenty of room for international tax planning designed to minimize domestic taxes by using Canadian-foreign affiliate company profit sharing and dividend distributions.

Offshore Shelter for You?

No one, probably including Revenue Canada, knows for sure how many Canadians now have established - or are about to establish - some form of offshore tax shelter.

But there definitely has been a rush of offshore-bound taxpayers, as indicated by booming attendance at tax haven seminars, sales of books on the subject - and the number of foreign bankers suddenly seeking Canadian business. Every increase in the tax rates means another layer of upper income taxpayers finds it affordable to recoup their tax losses by setting up an offshore tax savings mechanism.

As we have noted, among the several foreign jurisdictions that are popular tax-shelter destinations for Canadians are Barbados, the Cayman Islands, the Turks and Caicos - all sunny Caribbean favorites, and European choices including Ireland, the Netherlands and the Channel Islands. All of these foreign bailiwicks have exceptionally low tax rates on corporate and personal income earned by foreign nationals, as well as other attractions to make them economically feasible for offshore Canadian operations.

As we have already said, going offshore is not cheap. Start-up and annual operating costs can be considerable, depending on the form of shelter employed. Before you decide, these costs must be realistically calculated against tax savings and other expenses - including the possible need to defend your tax shelter against attack by Revenue Canada. But if you can cut your taxes by half, that should finance much of your initial cost, and after that the net results will be like receiving an annual bonus.

Tax Haven or "Sham"?

There are four very basic rules of the game concerning offshore tax shelters laid down by Canadian law - and strictly enforced by Revenue Canada.

These rules apply to any offshore tax shelters - either corporations or trusts, including the immigrant trust - and are aimed at abuse of such operations.

1. Residence.
A corporation or a trust, even though created in a foreign country under that country's laws, whose effective management is in Canada, will be taxed on its entire income and capital gains as if it were resident in Canada. This goes for a section 94 immigration trust as well.

To avoid this rule, actual control and management must be located within the foreign country, and all legal formalities supporting this status must be observed. A Canadian citizen is not prevented from being a shareholder, officer or director of an offshore company under this rule - but proven majority foreign control, on paper and in fact, is essential.

2. Artificiality. Except in the case of an immigrant trust, there must be a demonstrably credible reason for the operations of the corporation or trust in the foreign country - other than mere tax avoidance. Otherwise Revenue Canada will hold it to be a "sham" and impose taxes as on any Canadian resident. This means there must be a legitimate purpose, a functioning business, a board of directors, an office and staff and all the other trappings of corporate life.

When there is a legitimate business purpose, there will be no Canadian taxes on any income from a corporation based in a tax haven country, until it is actually paid to the Canadian resident in the form of salary or dividends. There is no penalty for accumulation of capital in the foreign company, and no rules which require its distribution.

This means that until the Canadian owner needs money for his or her use, or until they sell the foreign business, taxes on these earnings can be deferred indefinitely - even for decades. Owners who want the money right away can be paid dividends, on which the Canadian tax is 36 percent, well below the income tax rate of 50 percent plus.

Using Canada as a Stepping Stone

It is worth underscoring that if a Canadian corporation has a foreign affiliate company in a country where Canada has a reciprocal tax agreement (nearly sixty nations are now listed by RC), any dividends paid out of the affiliate's exempt surplus (essentially meaning profits from current income), will be tax free if paid in Canada to a corporate shareholder.

For example, a foreign affiliate located in Ireland, manufacturing for export to the United Kingdom, and enjoying a tax holiday under liberal Irish business incentive laws, or a Barbados, Cyprus or Jamaican foreign affiliate qualifying under the domestic tax incentive laws of those nations - can easily generate surplus dividends not taxable in Canada to a Canadian corporate shareholder - a major and very profitable tax savings in many instances.

Dividends paid by a tax haven affiliate company to a Canadian corporate shareholder are treated as exempt surplus and are tax free to the Canadian company - a major boon for tax planning and tax reduction. Interest and royalties paid between two such affiliated companies are also tax free.

For example, loan interest paid by a U.S. affiliate to a Canadian company is subject to a 15 percent gross tax - but the same U.S. payment routed through a Netherlands Antilles affiliate corporation to its Canadian affiliate company, would be tax free. It is worth noting in this regard that Canada does not tax foreign affiliates which are in fact holding companies.

3. "FAPI": In order to regulate offshore financial activity by individual Canadians, in 1976 the federal government promulgated the "Foreign Accrual Property Income" rules - known fondly to Revenue Canada and accountants as "FAPI". The FAPI bottom line requires reporting on income tax forms <u>any</u> "foreign accrual property income," especially "passive" income from offshore investments of any kind.

This is so, even if the income is not transferred back to Canada, even if the money only accumulates abroad in a foreign trust or corporate account. Depending on the applicable provision of law, such foreign income may or may not be taxable - but regardless of any tax liability, every dollar of it must be reported.

Personal foreign accrual property income not only must be reported, but certain types of FAPI (as defined by law) from a Canadian-controlled foreign corporate affiliate, and from certain specified foreign trusts, is taxable currently to Canadian shareholders or trust beneficiaries, whether or not that income is actually remitted to Canada. This covers Canadian investors, regardless of how many shares they own, who have passive interests in offshore investment corporations. While the entire actual net profit of the offshore investment company is not taxed proportionally to each shareholder, there is a complicated RC formula which apportions annual tax liability.

Together with annual FAPI reporting requirements, this annual offshore investment tax has dampened Canadian enthusiasm for foreign ventures devoted solely to producing investment income. Again, FAPI does not apply to a qualified immigrant trust.

4. Inter-company Pricing. Tax haven companies created solely for <u>importing</u> into Canada are subjected to full Canadian taxes. In addition, there can be no overpricing charged by a foreign parent company, for example, for exporting goods from its Canadian subsidiary for international sales. Overpricing has been a popular but illegal tactic used in an attempt to shift capital from parent companies in high tax Canada to the low tax haven affiliate. RC has gone to court repeatedly to challenge such schemes, albeit with mixed results.

In cases of offshore trading, entailing the activities of a Canadian affiliated tax haven company transferring goods between two other countries, RC authorities always watch very closely - and often conduct annual audits. Even if the tax haven company survives the RC residency and sham tests, it may fail the inter-company pricing regulations, especially if Canada is involved as one leg of the shipping triangle as an importer or exporter. Of course when Canada is "out of the loop," as when a Canadian affiliate company in the Channel Islands is shipping Scottish woolens to Europe, such pricing regulations do not apply - and nether do the taxes.

All this may sound complicated and discouraging but - it can be done!

In Conclusion

There you have it. It may seem a difficult road to travel, but becoming a Canadian citizen investor can save you and your heirs many millions of dollars that would otherwise go directly to the U.S. Internal Revenue Service.

Yes, these savings are predicated on major changes including surrender of your U.S. citizenship, moving your self, your family, and your business to Canada, and possible to another country later on - but the true "bottom line" measured in dollar savings can be enormous.

Most persons of wealth usually have considerable talent, a keen sense of adventure and shrewd judgment when it comes to money. And if such people chose the Canadian immigration route, they will earn and retain a lot more wealth than could otherwise be theirs.

Go Do It!

Consider what your world might be like should you be given the power to do exactly what you wanted to do with your life.

We ask you to dream. Expand your personal horizons to include all the world — not the limited world you may have known most, or all, of your life — but the world beyond and all its infinite possibilities.

One of history's greatest despots, the Corsican, Napoleon Bonaparte, is reported to have said: "Imagination rules the world." And perhaps, in his imagination (but, thank God, only there) he fulfilled that self-anointed destiny.

We are far more indebted to G. K. Chesterton for his practical wisdom: "The centre of every man's existence is a dream." If Chesterton's observation was not entirely accurate, we can only wish it could be, at least as it applies to our lives.

We hope we have offered for your serious consideration the kinds of information which will spur you on to fulfill your dream — whatever it may be — and wherever it may lead you — as a citizen of the world.

About the Author

Adam Starchild is the author of over twenty books, and hundreds of magazine articles, primarily on business and finance. His articles have a appeared in a wide range of publications around the world — including *Business Credit, Euromoney, Finance, The Financial Planner, International Living, Offshore Financial Review, Reason, Tax Planning International, Trusts & Estates, World Trade*, and many more.

His personal website on the Internet is at http://www.cyberhaven.com/starchild/